Decoding the Golf Swing Plane

Decoding the GOLF SWING PLANE

The Striking Plane Swing Model

First Edition

XICHAO MO

with Dan Courtney

DECODING THE GOLF SWING PLANE
COPYRIGHT ©2014 BY XICHAO MO

FIRST EDITION

May, 2014

ISBN-13: 978-0-692-21708-5
ISBN-10: 0-692-21708-8

Editor: Jacqueline Courtney
Interior Models: Dan Courtney, Xichao Mo, Curtis Metcalf,
        Sean Dunn, Andrew Arbesfeld, Cynthia & Derek Mo
Front Cover Photo: Dan Courtney

Paclinx PACLINX PUBLISHING
Special discount may be available for bulk orders from businesses or educational institutions. Please email: sales@paclinx.com for more details. More information on this and future golf books can also be found at the following website: www.golfswingselftraining.com

To My Dear Family

CONTENTS

ACKNOWLEDGEMENTS

I would like to express my sincere appreciation to all the lovely people who have kindly supported and positively influenced this book and the research project it was based on.

The most special appreciation goes to my ten-year-old boy Derek, who is the original inspiration for the project, for his persistent motivation and loyal support; also to my wife Hua and daughter Cynthia for their wonderful job in proofreading.

Jacqueline Courtney, a public affairs specialist and military journalist with the Missouri National Guard, did an outstanding job editing and proofreading most of the manuscript by sparing time from her very busy schedule. She demonstrated impressive editing skills and is very pleasant to work with. I am deeply indebted to Jacqueline for her remarkable contribution.

I am very thankful to Tony Chung, a friend at GE Aviation, for introducing me to the game of golf and for his kind guidance in the first two years, and also to Judd Swanson at GE for his great swing tips.

My friends Curtis Metcalf, Andrew Arbesfeld, and Sean Dunn all did an excellent job modeling for this book. I want to thank them for demonstrating their extraordinary shotmaking skills and for their strong support.

I also want to compliment our beta readers, Dan Near, Leon Wang, Kerry Rennie, Jun Ma, and Ralph Paonessa, for their valuable comments. Leon Wang provided me with many insightful and detailed suggestions. His knowledge in golf is impressive and his efforts are much appreciated.

Sherry Meltzer, Ken West, Ed Lamont, Diana Loy, Alexandra Van Horn, and other wonderful people at the Palm Beach Noon Toastmaster Club, thank you all for your inspiration and feedback.

Over the years, I have also learned many useful things from several golf teachers in south Florida and I am certainly grateful to their kind help: Randi Oetting, Fred Stone, Chad Kurmel, and Mike Walsh.

Last but not least, I would like to extend my appreciation to co-author Dan Courtney, an ambitious young player and a talented instructor at Cypress Creek Country Club, Florida, for his positive influence on my swing and research. Dan has also provided valuable feedback on the project and modeled for many of the swing videos and pictures, including the one on the front cover.

INTRODUCTION

We all know how important the swing plane is to our games, just as Ben Hogan had said more than half a century ago, "Learning to think in terms of this plane has helped tremendously to improve and stabilize the swings of many friends of mine."

However, when your game constantly drives you crazy and you have no idea what is wrong, does it ever occur to you that the swing plane theory you have learned is wrong?

In fact, with a very high probability it is. Here is the shocking truth: *a swing plane by its popular definition does not even exist!*

What you have learned about the swing plane might have hurt your game. This is not an exaggeration; it is a fact supported by what I have seen in various golf media over the past several years.

As of today, there is no standard on swing plane theories in the golf community. Instead, there are many conflicting ideas. Most of the theories do not match what actually happens in a real golf swing. In my opinion, this is largely due to an interesting phenomenon in golf: what people see and feel is often different from what is actually done. Style and essence are often disconnected. No wonder we often see that a guy with an "ugly" swing plays a better game than one with a "good looking" swing.

In this book, I will discuss the essence of the golf swing plane and the fundamental principles of club movement, which have been summarized from the swings of many great ball strikers in history through extensive research and analyses.

These true swing plane fundamentals, which I call the "swing secret in plain sight" can be seen in the swings of all great golfers and easily verified through video analyses.

These fundamentals will be presented in this book as an easy-to-understand model, which is supported by the theory of classical mechanics and the knowledge of human anatomy. The *Striking Plane Swing Model*, as it is called, will help golfers of all levels better understand the essence of swing plane and further improve their ball striking skills.

The model can be easily validated using the swing of any great player in history and has been successfully used to analyze and improve the swings of golfers of different skill levels. It is also confirmed that players with unorthodox swings can hit great shots as long as they follow these fundamentals.

The model itself is very simple, although the background information in the first few chapters might be a little technical. Understanding the background information is not mandatory but can be highly rewarding. This is especially true for chapter four, *the upright posture swing,* which looks at the swing plane and club movement from an intuitive point of view. This new perspective releases our natural potentials in targeting objects and makes things much easier to understand.

With a thorough understanding of the swing plane fundamentals, a golfer's ability to judge will improve. He will no longer blindly follow every tip or instruction that is taught to him; he will be able to diagnose his own swing issues and work more effectively with his instructors.

A golfer who truly understands the swing plane will eventually gain the ultimate freedom in the game. He will no longer be restricted by textbook instructions. He will be able to create his own swing by tweaking the non-essential elements while adhering to the true fundamentals. He will swing with his own style and play at a different level, just as Arnold Palmer puts it, "Swing your swing."

1. THE SWING PLANE

Without a doubt, the swing plane is one of the most talked about topics among golfers, both professionals and amateurs. In the world of golf, people simply couldn't avoid the discussion of the swing plane, just like they couldn't stop talking about Tiger Woods. If a golfer hasn't heard about the swing plane, we can almost be sure that he hasn't been involved in the game long enough or seriously enough. The truth is: swing plane is not just another buzz word; it is indeed a very important concept in the game.

WHAT IS A SWING PLANE?

What exactly is a swing plane? In the game of golf, a swing plane refers to a flat surface along which a golfer moves his club in the process of hitting a ball. The key word here is *flat*, which many people conveniently ignore. We will talk more about this later.

The concept of the golf swing plane is not new; it has been around since the early 20th century. In the 1920s, Seymour Dunn, a golf teacher in New York and the author of *Golf Fundamentals*, put together a swing training aid with wood framing and canvas. The aid was like an oversized painting canvas with an oval cutout in the middle and was used to demonstrate how a club should move in a golf swing. A golfer was supposed to stand behind the canvas, stick his head and upper body through the cutout, and swing his club along the surface of the canvas plane.

This type of swing plane trainer would certainly do a decent job in getting a student to swing his club in a more orderly form (instead of some random movements). Unfortunately, it wouldn't be highly effective because it was based on a fundamentally incorrect swing model. We will talk more about this in the following chapters.

Fig. 1-1 A Canvas Swing Plane Trainer

Although the concept of the swing plane was introduced by Seymour Dunn (and perhaps other people) much earlier, it didn't get popular until golf legend Ben Hogan published his bestselling book, *Five Lessons, the Modern Fundamentals of Golf*, in 1957.

In this classic golf book, Mr. Hogan presented the most influential image of a golf swing plane: a huge pane of glass, with a cutout for his head to stick out, resting on his shoulders. Even today, plenty of golf instructors are still using the shoulder plane line as the key reference in their swing analyses.

The swing plane image from Ben Hogan helped millions of golfers establish a mental road map for their club movement. Instead of looping the club wildly, golfers started to swing their clubs along a surface inclined at a specific angle.

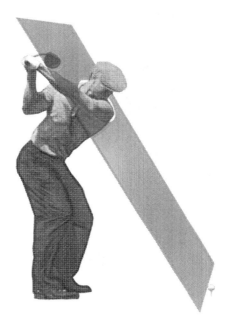

Fig. 1-2 Ben Hogan's Swing Plane

Today, nearly six decades after it was first published, *Five Lessons* is still the swing bible for millions of golfers. It is also the number one bestselling golf instruction book on the market.

WHY IS THE SWING PLANE SO IMPORTANT?

Why do golfers even care about the swing plane? Why couldn't we just pick up the club and hit the ball the way we hammer a nail or chop down a tree? The answer is simple: golf is a game that rewards ball striking accuracy, consistency, and power. The swing plane, if used properly, can help us acquire these qualities and become better golfers.

A long time ago, golfers have figured out that the result of a shot has a lot to do with the way a club moves before it touches the ball. The swing path of the club determines whether or not the clubhead can be returned precisely behind the ball with the

3

momentum pointing to the right direction, and therefore will affect the quality of a shot.

The swing plane to a golf swing is like the route for a mountain trip. If you have the correct road map, you will be able to choose the right route and arrive at your destination safely and efficiently. If you ever get lost, a good road map can help you get back on track. Without it, you could fail the mission or even put yourself in danger.

A swing plane model is the road map for club movement in a golf swing. If you learn the right swing plane model and follow it properly, your shots can be more predictable and your game can become more consistent.

Just as Mr. Hogan had said, "Learning to think in terms of this plane has helped tremendously to improve and stabilize the swings of many friends of mine. It seems to induce a golfer to make the correct backswing movements TIME AFTER TIME."

THE CONFUSION

As important as it is, swing plane is also the most misunderstood concept among golfers, including amateurs, tour players, and even teaching professionals.

Many golfers believe they have a perfect understanding of the swing plane and might disagree with the statement above. After all, the swing plane is not rocket science; it is such a simple and straightforward concept.

Unfortunately, the statement is true and can be easily backed up with a wealth of evidence from various golf books, magazines, and instructional videos. I am confident that you will agree with my assessment after reading the facts and examples in the following chapters.

There is an interesting phenomenon in golf: *what people think they are doing often differs from what they are actually doing.* If you are a golf instructor or have seen your own swing in the video, then you certainly know what this means. Our perception and sensation can sometimes be deceptive.

In the case of the swing plane, many golfers believe they swing their clubs on a plane that doesn't actually exist.

Just like many other amateur golfers, I have gone through the various stages of learning the swing plane. I had no idea what a swing plane was in the first year or two until I heard about it from golf instructor David Leadbetter's DVD. After reading Ben Hogan's *Five Lessons*, I thought I had learned everything I ever needed to know about the swing plane. Nothing could be simpler; it is just a pane of glass resting on your shoulders.

I was terribly wrong.

One day, I stumbled into a local golf store and ended up getting a swing analysis at its golf academy. I was quite surprised when the instructor, Dan, pointed out that my takeaway was too much inside. After reviewing the video with him, I had to plead guilty. I also found out my perception for the club position was not as good as I thought. When I felt my club was aligned properly, it was actually laid off quite a bit. That wasn't a great day for my self-confidence.

Garden Stick

Plywood Panel

Adjustable Stand

Fig. 1-3 My Homemade Swing Plane Trainer

To fix my takeaway, I built a swing plane trainer (as shown in Fig. 1-3) using a piece of plywood and a few hinges I got from Home Depot. This training aid worked wonderfully and soon I was very happy with my takeaway.

I then decided to go a step further and use the trainer to check my full swing. That was when I noticed something strange. At the top of the backswing, I realized my club was not on the plywood plane at all; instead, it was way above it. I was aware of the fact that the plane at impact could be different from, and usually is a little steeper than, that at setup. However, after I had adjusted the plane guide to the impact angle, the club was still noticeably above the plane even when it came down half way.

Apparently the club wasn't moving on a plane all the time. That was different from what I had learned. What was going on?

The club is still above the
plane half way in downswing

Downswing   Impact

Fig. 1-4 Club Positions

THE ANSWER

Being an inquisitive engineer, I was determined to find out the reason behind it. After staring at the computer screen for a couple of weeks and watching hundreds of swing videos of the tour players, I noticed something interesting: all great players have some common features in their swings regardless of their styles. After some experiments in the garage, I believed I found the answer to my question.

In addition, I was quite happy to find out that the advanced physics I studied at college was not a total waste of time. All these common features could be conveniently explained using the laws and principles of classical mechanics, which was established by the great English scientist Isaac Newton back in the 17th century as a branch of the physics.

These common features exist universally in the swings of all great players, including the older generation golfers, such as Ben Hogan and Arnold Palmer, and the modern tour players, such as Tiger Woods and Adam Scott. They can also be seen in the swings of those golfers with unique and unconventional styles, such as Moe Norman and Jim Furyk.

To my surprise, these fundamental features are not complicated at all. However, they can easily elude a pair of untrained eyes because of the seeming simplicity of the swing plane.

I also found it hard to believe that these swing plane fundamentals, which all great players have physically followed, have rarely been discussed systematically in the publications available to average golfers. In fact, very few of the bestselling golf books, other than Ben Hogan's *Five Lessons*, had touched the topic of swing plane extensively. Perhaps the swing plane concept might have seemed too simple and too straightforward to many golfers that no elaboration was deemed necessary. Since the professionals universally execute these fundamentals, it had been my suspicion that there was a "hidden manual" somewhere for the tour pros.

Today, the majority of the amateur golfers are still in desperate need of true and tested swing theories that can really help them better understand the golf swing, especially the swing plane, so their journey of game improvement can be more enjoyable and less frustrating.

At present, there are several swing plane theories and models in circulation, but there is barely any that is compatible with the real world golf swing.

It is not an understatement that the poor understanding of the swing plane has contributed to the frustration that millions of average golfers are suffering from, and has affected the healthy growth of the golf industry. A correct swing plane model can and will make learning golf more fun and game improvement more effective.

In the follow chapters, I will discuss these common features and the golf swing "road map" I summarized: *the Striking Plane Swing Model*.

Please be advised that this model is not about a new way to swing a golf club; rather, it simply identifies and describes the fundamental characteristics that already exist in the swings of all great players. It is an effort to bring to your attention the swing plane "secret" that has always been in plain sight.

2. Swing Plane Basics

Many things in the golf world have yet to be standardized and the golf terminology is definitely one of them. Before we begin our in-depth and exciting discussions on the golf swing plane and the new model, it would be beneficial to clarify the definitions of the important terms we will be using in the following chapters and do a quick review on the existing swing plane theories.

What is a Plane?

The word *plane* has been used very loosely in the golf community. Since it is a critical term and will be referred to repeatedly in the rest of the book, we shall all understand its proper definition.

In very simple language, a plane is a flat surface, either real or imaginary. For example, the surface of the big mirror in your bathroom is flat, and therefore is a plane. If the mirror had an uneven surface, you would look funny in it. On the other hand, a curved surface, whether smooth or rough, shall not be called a plane. For instance, the windshield of a Ferrari sports car is typically not a plane. It usually has a streamlined, curvy, and smooth surface in order to reduce wind resistance at high speeds.

As a more precise definition, a plane is a surface that meets the following criterion: if a straight line is drawn to connect ANY two points on the surface, then every point of the straight line will be on that surface. There is no need to worry if you find this definition a little technical. All we need to know is that a plane is flat.

CLUBHEAD PLANE AND SHAFT PLANE

We are going to explain a key principle in this section. Readers can go directly to the conclusion if the explanation sounds too technical.

If the path the clubhead travels along belongs to a flat surface, we will call this surface the *clubhead plane*. In a typical full swing, the entire clubhead path doesn't usually fit on a plane, although a certain section of it may.

If the surface the shaft travels on is a plane, we will call it the *shaft plane*. When the shaft moves on a plane, then every part of it, including the clubhead, is also on the same plane.

In Fig. 2-1, a club is perpendicular to a vertical axis and rotating around it. The whole club is moving on the same horizontal plane.

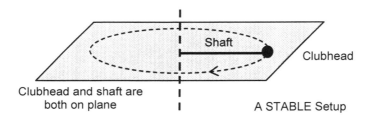

Fig. 2-1 The Shaft Moves on a Plane

From a technical point of view, this coplanar setup is stable. No matter how fast the club rotates, it has a tendency to stay on the same plane. If the clubhead hits a ball head-on while rotating, it won't be knocked out of the plane by the impact torque.

However, if the clubhead is moving on a plane, it does not necessarily mean the shaft is. This can be demonstrated by the setup shown in Fig. 2-2. With the club rotating around a vertical axis at a sharp angle, the clubhead moves along a circular path that fits on a horizontal plane. However, the shaft travels on a cone-shaped surface that is outside of the clubhead plane.

This setup is not intrinsically stable. As the shaft rotates faster, the clubhead has a tendency to rise higher and the angle between the shaft and the vertical axis will get closer to 90 degrees.

10

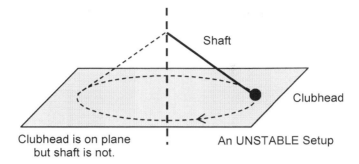

Shaft

Clubhead

Clubhead is on plane but shaft is not.

An UNSTABLE Setup

Fig. 2-2 The Shaft is outside of the Clubhead Plane

You can observe this phenomenon by spinning a string with a fishing weight attached to the end (Fig. 2-3). The faster the weight spins, the higher it rises.

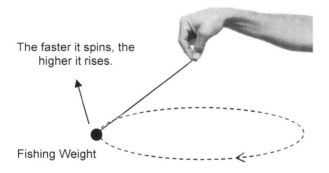

The faster it spins, the higher it rises.

Fishing Weight

Fig. 2-3 Fishing Weight Spinning Experiment

With the setup in Fig. 2-2, the shaft flexes when the clubhead strikes a ball as a result of the impact torque. The bending will take the clubhead out of its original swing plane and may alter the ball launch direction.

Here is the conclusion: *when the entire club swings on plane, it is more stable and easier to manage. It will deliver shots that are more predictable and consistent.*

THE SETUP SHAFT PLANE

Now we are going to define two important terms. A professional golfer typically sets up to a ball with a conventional posture, as shown in Fig. 2-4. From a side view, the golfer's arms and the club are NOT on a straight line in a conventional setup.

At the setup position, the club shaft and the target line together define a plane, which will be referred to as the *Setup Shaft Plane* (SSP) in this book. From a proper view facing the target, the SSP would appear as a straight line running along the club shaft.

The SSP is not a swing plane because the golf club doesn't necessarily travel on it during an actual swing. It mainly serves as a reference plane in swing analyses, and is a term frequently used in the following chapters.

Unconventional

Conventional

Fig. 2-4 The Setup Shaft Plane (SSP)

THE NORMAL STRIKING PLANE

At the moment of impact, the clubhead returns behind the ball. At this point, the club shaft and the target line together define a very

12

important reference plane, which is called the *Normal Striking Plane* (NSP), as shown in Fig. 2-5. This is the plane a club shall travel on within the impact zone in order to hit a pure straight shot.

Careful readers might have noticed that the shaft bends downwards slightly as the clubhead approaching the ball so it is impossible to draw a straight line along it. This phenomenon is caused by the fact that the center of gravity (COG) of the clubhead is not in line with the shaft. During a high speed swing, the clubhead has a tendency to move towards the shaft plane and causes the shaft to flex. The proper way to define the NSP is to draw a line from the grip to the sweet spot of the clubface, as shown in Fig. 2-5.

Since the shaft does not necessarily return to its setup plane at impact, the NSP can be, and usually is, different from the SSP.

In this book, the plane that a club actually travels on within the impact zone is called the *striking plane* (KP), which ideally would be the NSP in a pure and straight shot. However, the KP and NSP could be different for a fade or a draw shot.

Fig. 2-5 The Normal Striking Plane (NSP)

The NSP is the most critical geometric reference in a golf swing. It is the *key reference plane*. From the viewpoint of physics, it is necessary for the club to swing on a plane to deliver a powerful, predictable, and accurate strike. As a matter of fact, all great ball strikers swing their clubs strictly on a plane within the impact zone.

13

Unless otherwise specified, we will assume a golfer's intention is to hit a pure straight shot and therefore would swing his club along the NSP within the impact zone.

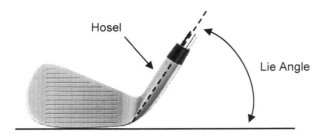

Fig. 2-6 The Lie Angle of a Club

Ideally, the angle of the NSP is the *lie angle* of the club being used (Fig. 2-6). In order to hit the ball solid, the NSP should be fairly close to the SSP. For this reason, once a golfer sets up to a ball, the angle of his NSP is relatively determined. For the majority of professional players, the NSP is normally a few (4~7) degrees steeper than the SSP, as shown in Fig. 2-7. This is due to the posture change at impact: the upper body is open and the left shoulder is away from its setup position (Fig.2-8).

Fig. 2-7 SSP and NSP are Different

14

Left shoulder
moves up and
back at impact

Fig. 2-8 Posture Change from Setup to Impact

Fig. 2-9 SSP and NSP are Identical

Although not commonly seen, some players, including Ben Hogan, Moe Norman, Vijay Singh, and Sergio Garcia, do return their clubs back to the SSP at impact. To do this, these players have to make extra posture adjustments to make solid contacts.

15

THE IMPACT ZONE

The area below a golfer's hips is the critical zone where the club is released and the ball striking action executed. Although I personally think it is more appropriate to call this area the striking zone, this book will continue using the legacy term *impact zone* due to its popularity. Please keep in mind that the *impact zone* may mean different things for different people. In this book, the impact zone specifically refers to the area below the golfer's hips, as shown in Fig. 2-10.

Fig. 2-10   The Impact Zone

SWING POSITIONS

To facilitate future discussions, we will define several commonly-used swing positions so all readers can be on the same page. Here we will use the golfer's left arm to define the swing positions for both the backswing and downswing.

From the setup to the top of a full swing, a golfer's left arm typically rotates about 140 degrees. By dividing this angle into four portions, we will have four swing positions, as shown in Fig. 2-11. The left arm angle for each position is approximate in the pictures. The main purpose is to establish some reference points.

16

Full Swing
Quarter-swing

Three-Quarter Swing
Half-swing

Fig. 2-11 Common Swing Positions

17

Inside vs. Outside

In the discussion of golf swing plane and club movement, the words *inside* and *outside* have specific meanings. Contrary to what many instructors have suggested, the outside and inside spaces are not separated by a vertical wall along the target line.

Technically, inside should actually refer to the space below the Normal Striking Plane (NSP), whereas outside refers to the space above. The club should move on the NSP around impact for a pure straight shot, not in-square-in as taught by some instructors. A club can be on the golfer side of the target line and still be outside the NSP, as shown in Fig. 2-12.

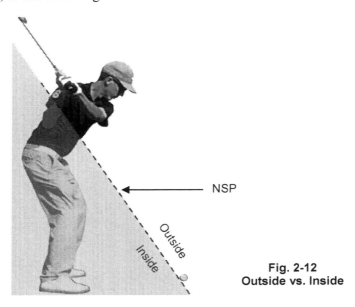

← NSP

Outside

Inside

**Fig. 2-12
Outside vs. Inside**

Existing Swing Plane Models and Theories

At present, several swing plane theories or models are being taught in the golf community. For background information, we are going to take a quick look at the common ones.

THE ROBOT SWING PLANE MODEL

As a passionate golfer, you must have heard about Iron Byron the swing robot, or at least have watched the hilarious European Tour commercial, in which Rory McIlroy challenged "Jeff" the Golf Laboratory Computer-Controlled Hitting Machine.

To accurately evaluate the performance of golf clubs, shafts, and balls, equipment testers must be able to eliminate the variables in the swings and consistently repeat certain shots. Obviously, a human golfer, no matter how great he is, would not be able to meet the stringent requirements. That was the reason why people decided to design and use electromechanical hitting machines, i.e. swing robots, for such demanding tasks.

The most famous swing robot, Iron Byron, was designed in the early 1960s for True Temper by George Manning and his team in Battelle Memorial Institute, Ohio.

Fig. 2-13 The Robot-style Swing Plane Model

The machine was named after legendary golfer Byron Nelson, who won 18 tournaments in 1945 and was famous for his ball striking consistency. These machines have been used by the USGA (United States Golf Association), as well as many leading golf equipment manufacturers, to test golf clubs and balls. Iron Byron's swing was so accurate and consistent that it had caused significant damage to the center strip of the USGA test fairway, which had to be repaired frequently.

Iron Byron is an admirable golfing machine with superior precision and consistency. It has a simple but ideal swing plane model which features the following characteristics:

1. The club moves on one plane throughout the backswing.
2. The club moves on one plane throughout the downswing.
3. The downswing plane is identical to the backswing plane.

The robot-style swing is a true one-plane swing (different from Jim Hardy's definition), meaning the club stays on a particular plane throughout the entire swing. There is no plane switching between the backswing and the downswing. It is simple, elegant, and consistent.

Without question, Iron Byron has the perfect swing every golfer dreams of. It is not surprising that many golf instructors have even tried to teach their human students the robot-style swing plane. These instructors believe that the club could be swung on a single plane by a human golfer, and that it should either point to the target line or be parallel to it at any point of a swing.

Unfortunately, they fail to realize that human beings are different from robots. A human golfer has a more complex anatomy, which gives him both flexibilities and limitations. As we will discuss later, although not completely impossible, it is quite uncomfortable and challenging for a human golfer to execute the robot-style one-plane swing.

BEN HOGAN'S SWING PLANE MODEL

In his famous book *Five Lessons*, Ben Hogan presented a highly influential swing plane model, which had been, and perhaps still is, the swing plane standard for numerous instructors and golfers.

Unlike the one-plane model featured in the robot-style golf swing, the backswing plane and downswing plane are different in Ben Hogan's model.

20

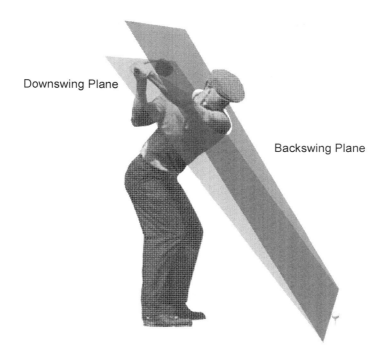

Fig. 2-14 Ben Hogan's Swing Plane Model

According to Ben Hogan, the backswing plane is like a pane of glass running from the ball to the top of the golfer's shoulders at setup. The golfer should keep his club under this plane all the time during the backswing. As his arms move higher than the hip level, they should remain *parallel* to the plane all the way to the top, where his left arm should extend at the *exact same angle* of the glass and brush against it (*Five Lessons*, page 79).

In the downswing, however, the golfer switches to a different plane, which inclines at a narrower angle than the backswing plane and points slightly to the right side of the target. According to Ben Hogan, this is because the plane still rests on the golfer's shoulders and the lateral weight shift causes his right shoulder to drop and the downswing plane to sink and shift (*Five Lessons*, page 87).

In summary, the features of Ben Hogan's swing plane model are as follows:

1. During the backswing, the club moves *under* a plane that rests on the golfer's shoulders.
2. During the downswing, the club moves *on* a downswing plane that also rests on the golfer's shoulders.
3. The downswing plane inclines at a shallower angle than the backswing plane

Although Mr. Hogan correctly described the feel of the downswing (the club drops to a lower plane), some of his statements didn't exactly match his action. This can be confirmed by analyzing his swing using software programs. I will point out a few areas for the readers to review.

First, Mr. Hogan did not actually swing his club back along the "backswing plane" (i.e. the shoulder plane) he described. During the backswing, his club moved up along the SSP, which is much lower than the "backswing plane," most of the time. His left arm did not brush against the "backswing plane" or extend at the exact same angle at the top of a full backswing. Neither did it maintain a parallel relation to this "backswing plane" after passing the hips.

Secondly, his actual downswing plane (or his actual striking plane by our definition in this book) did not rest on his shoulders. Instead, it passed through his waist level and was the same as his SSP. Apparently, Mr. Hogan thought he was swinging down on a plane resting on his shoulders but actually was not.

Thirdly, Mr. Hogan's club didn't travel on a plane throughout the entire downswing. At the top, his club was above the actual downswing plane (striking plane), and didn't get on the plane until it arrived at the half-swing position.

We will analyze Mr. Hogan's swing more thoroughly in chapter seven. You are also encouraged to check into the areas mentioned above with your own tools.

Nonetheless, Mr. Hogan correctly described what a proper swing should feel like, and his swing plane model has inspired millions of golfers to improve their games using this important concept. Compared to the robot-style model, his theory is a step forward in describing the human golf swing.

HANK HANEY'S SWING PLANE MODEL

Golf instructor Hank Haney is one of the people who have made noticeable efforts in studying the swing plane theory and he certainly sees things many other instructors have ignored.

In his book *The Only Golf Lesson You'll Ever Need*, Hank Haney devoted 15 pages to the discussion of a unique swing plane model, which he called the congruent-angle swing plane. This book is one of the few publications that actually discuss the swing plane in detail besides Ben Hogan's *Five Lessons*.

Unlike many other instructors, Mr. Haney thinks the club does not actually move on one plane during a swing, instead, it moves through many planes, which are all parallel to the SSP. Although not in total agreement with his theory, I do believe there are valid points in it. Recognizing the fact that a club does not move on plane the entire time is a step closer to the truth.

The key points of Hank Haney's swing plane model can be summarized as follows:

1. The setup shaft angle (down-the-line view) determines the swing plane angle.
2. The club moves up through a series of planes, which are parallel to the SSP, during the entire backswing.
3. The club moves down through the same series of parallel planes on its way to the impact position during the downswing
4. At impact, the club returns to its setup shaft angle.

According to Mr. Haney, the club is considered off-plane if at any point its shaft is not parallel to the SSP. He states that a steep or flat swing can be achieved by moving the club at an angle steeper or flatter than its setup shaft angle.

Fig. 2-15 Hank Haney's Swing Plane Model

In this model, Mr. Haney offered additional insight on the actual club movement and observed something Ben Hogan didn't realize or discuss. His swing plane model and the one to be introduced in this book share some similarities in certain area. For example, both recognize the fact that a golfer is not capable of keeping the club on one plane throughout a conventional full swing.

Hank Haney's swing plane model made some improvement over Ben Hogan's. However, it also includes claims that are not fundamental and leaves the mechanical essence of a sound golf swing undefined.

There are at least three major areas in his model that are considered arguable, in addition to many other supporting statements.

First, the majority of the modern tour players do not return their clubs to the setup shaft plane. Tiger Woods, whom Hank Haney had previously coached for many years, never returns his club to the setup shaft plane; neither does Mark O'meara, Haney's long time student.

Secondly, this model emphasizes the importance of keeping the shaft parallel to the setup shaft plane during the entire backswing and downswing, but fails to explain why players like Jim Furyk and Jack Nicklaus can deviate from this major principle of the model and still hit great shots.

Thirdly, Mr. Haney did not specifically describe the club movement within the critical area of a golf swing: the impact zone. It is not clear whether he suggests the club should still move through a series of parallel planes inside this area.

JIM HARDY'S SWING THEORY

Golf instructor Jim Hardy introduced some fresh concepts in his book *The Plane Truth for Golfers*, which has triggered intense discussions and controversial opinions on his "one-plane" and "two-plane" swing concepts.

Mr. Hardy believes that a golfer can be categorized as either a "one-plane" or a "two-plane" swinger; and that each person should use the style that is more suitable for his physique.

Although Mr. Hardy's theory made an effort in differentiating swing styles, it did not systematically define the essence of the swing plane or the principles for club movements. It is, therefore, not a swing plane model in my opinion.

Mr. Hardy gave arguable definitions to the one-plane and two-plane swings. In fact, a human golfer's shoulders barely move on a plane when he swings with a club in his hands, because his left shoulder gradually moves higher above the original shoulder plane during the backswing. Furthermore, the shoulder plane and the arm plane, even being parallel to each other, are still considered two planes. So it seems the styles Mr. Hardy described could be more precisely called one-axis and two-axis swings.

In this book, one-plane swing refers to a swing in which the club moves up and down on the same plane the entire time, as in the robot-style swing. To avoid the confusion caused by the different definitions, Jim Hardy's definition will be referred to with quotation marks as "one-plane" in the rest of this book, unless specified otherwise.

WHAT ABOUT THE D-PLANE?

Many golfers have heard about the term D-plane. What is it exactly? Does it have anything to do with the swing plane?

D-plane is a concept mostly used in the analysis of ball flight. It is associated with the ball spin rather than the club movement. In a nutshell, D-plane describes how a ball would spin at launch. It is a plane where the equator of a spinning ball resides, or to which the ball spin axis is perpendicular to. It has no direct connection with the swing plane theories.

Readers who are interested in this concept can read more online. There are a lot of articles and videos on the internet discussing the D-plane, which is a confusing concept often explained in even more confusing ways. In my opinion, very few people explained it as well as golf teacher James Leitz did in one of his videos.

THE ROLE OF A SWING PLANE MODEL

A swing plane model to a golfer's game is just like a road map to a journey in the mountains. Learning the correct swing plane model is like getting an up-to-date road map or an experienced tour guide for your journey.

A golfer who lacks a thorough understanding of the swing plane essence can easily get lost in the flood of tips and quick fixes surrounding us today, since it is difficult for him to tell the truth from the nonsense,

With the guidance of a sound swing plane model, he will not only know *how* to move his club, but also understand *why* he should do it in certain ways. With the right knowledge, he will have a better chance successfully executing the shots he has in mind. He will also gain the ability to self-diagnose his own swings, and therefore can practice more intelligently and effectively.

Needless to say, knowing the correct swing plane model does not automatically earn you the US Open Championship. Knowing how something should be done is just the first step. You still need the strength, the will, and the hard work to accomplish your goals.

26

The difference is: the right knowledge gives you more power. It makes learning the game more fun. You will become a more intelligent golfer, and most importantly, a happier golfer.

3. THE HUMAN GOLF SWING

The human body is a highly advanced and sophisticated system, much more complicated than any machine ever built. Because of his unique anatomical structure, a human golfer usually swings a club in a style quite different from that of a robot. In this chapter, we will briefly review the unique nature of a typical human golf swing. Understanding the uniqueness and intrinsic limitations of the human body is critical to the discussion of the swing plane model in the following chapters.

THE MYTHS OF A HUMAN GOLF SWING

There are many myths about golf swings that golfers were taught to believe. Here are a few typical ones:

 Myth 1: The golf club moves on one plane throughout the entire backswing.

 Myth 2: The golf club moves on one plane throughout the entire downswing.

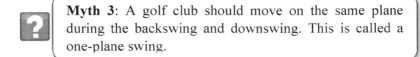

Myth 3: A golf club should move on the same plane during the backswing and downswing. This is called a one-plane swing.

Myth 4: The swing plane runs from the ball through the golfer's shoulders.

Myth 5: With the same club and the same setup, a golfer can still choose to swing on a steep or a flat swing plane.

Myth 6: The plane for the clubhead, which actually hits the ball, is what really matters in a golf swing. The shaft path is not relevant.

Myth 7: The club must return to its setup plane at impact.

Myths 1, 2, and 3 are considered true by many golfers and instructors, because they represent a simple, intuitive, and ideal swing model. In fact, that is how Iron Byron swings a club. Don't we all want to be as accurate and consistent as Iron Byron?

Mr. Hogan would probably endorse myth 2, but without question would reject myth 3; because he had stated that the downswing plane should incline at a shallower angle than the backswing plane.

Myths 4 and 5 are quite popular among golf teachers at various levels. Myths 6 and 7 are not as popular but are supported by some renowned instructors.

Here comes the shocking truth: *none of these myths is true for a conventional golf swing!*

THE TRUTH ABOUT THE SWING PLANE

As we all know, experiments are the best myth-busters. Let's do a simple experiment to find out what happens in a real golf swing.

We will play back a top tour player's swing video recorded at high speed from the golfer's right side (down-the-line view), and we will trace the club movement using a series of straight lines. Only a true slow motion video can provide enough frames for this experiment. A video recorded at a regular speed (30 frames per second) and then played back slowly will not provide enough details. The video used in this experiment was recorded from a proper angle so the club will appear to be moving along a straight line if it travels on the proper plane.

What do you think we will see?

Backswing   Downswing

Fig. 3-1 The Club Path in a Golf Swing

The surface the club travels on during the backswing is not a plane at all! Not even close. *Apparently, the "backswing plane" does not actually exist,* not in this modern textbook swing.

The surface the club travels on during the downswing is not a plane either; but it is better. Within the impact zone, which is the area below a golfer's hip level, the club is moving on a plane given a reasonable amount of tolerance. In this book, we will call this plane, on which the club actually travels within the impact zone during the downswing, the *striking plane*.

The brutal truth is: *the backswing plane and downswing plane do not exist in a conventional full swing*. The club only moves on plane near and within the impact zone. Only in a partial swing, such as a chipping or short pitching swing, can a club swing on one plane the entire time.

Even though a swing plane does not actually exist for a full swing, we will continue using this popular legacy term in some occasions to refer to the NSP or the striking plane.

KEEPING THE SHAFT ON PLANE

Some instructors have claimed that a golfer only needs to keep the clubhead moving on plane in a golf swing since it is the clubhead that actually hits the ball. They don't think having the shaft also on plane is relevant to ball striking. That is why these instructors promote swing plane trainers that focus on keeping the clubhead on plane, as shown in Fig. 3-2.

This claim might appear to make sense, but actually won't hold up in either theory or reality.

In theory, leaving the club shaft outside of the swing plane can cause stability issues especially during a high speed impact, as explained earlier in chapter two. The huge torque produced by the impact force through the long shaft will impede the clubhead movement and cause shaft bending. If the shaft and the clubhead are both moving on the same plane, the bending caused by a head-on impact also happens within the same plane and won't significantly alter the ball flight. Otherwise, the clubhead can be knocked out of its plane, causing change to the ball launch direction.

In reality, it would be very difficult, if at all possible, for a golfer to swing the club shaft on a curved surface and meanwhile keep the clubhead perfectly on plane. Even if it can be done, consistency would be a big issue.

That is why *every* great ball striker swings the entire club on plane within the impact zone, just as we see in Fig. 3-1. I haven't seen any great player who is an exception to this rule.

During the backswing and the early stage of the downswing, the shaft is not always moving on a plane, but it won't matter much at these stages since they are less critical and the swing speed is still low. Once inside the impact zone, the club accelerates and moves at a much higher speed. In this case, it is crucial to keep the whole club on plane to deliver stable, consistent, and accurate shots.

To summarize, what we should focus on in a golf swing is to *keep the whole club moving on plane within the high speed impact zone*. From this point on, when we talk about the swing plane, we refer to one on which the entire club, not just the clubhead, travels.

Many swing plane training aids, such as the ones shown in Fig. 3-2, are based on the idea of swinging only the clubhead on plane. These single-rail "swing plane" trainers will teach a student the wrong swing plane concept. They also suggest that the clubhead moves on a plane the entire time, which never actually happens in a real golf swing!

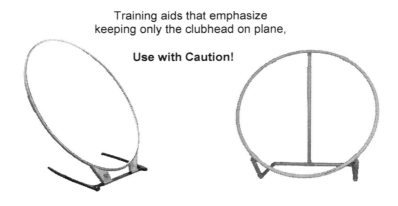

Training aids that emphasize
keeping only the clubhead on plane,

Use with Caution!

Fig. 3-2 Single-rail Swing Plane Training Aids

32

THE HUMAN ANATOMY

Since the robot-style one-plane swing is so accurate and efficient, we naturally want to ask a question: why couldn't the tour player swing the club like a robot and keep his club on plane all the time?

The answer lies in our special anatomical structure. A swing robot might have an extraordinarily consistent and precise swing, but that's all it can do: swinging a club. It is a mechanical device with a single function. A human body, on the other hand, can accomplish many other tasks and is therefore much more sophisticated.

A normal human body has one hip joint, two legs, two knees, two arms, two shoulders, two elbows, and two wrists, all of which are actively involved in a golf swing and make the process extremely complicated. Even a tiny mistake in coordination can result in a terrible shot.

The key joints involved in a golf swing are the hips, shoulders, elbows, and wrists. The shoulders are among the most flexible joints in the human body and have a great range of motion. The wrists and elbows, on the other hand, are much more restricted. A wrist moves like a hinge with a range of motion of about 180 degrees.

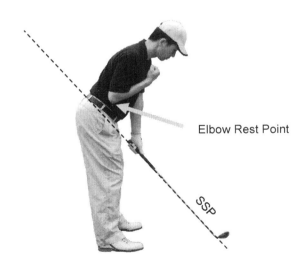

Elbow Rest Point

SSP

Fig. 3-3 The Elbow Rest Point

The anatomical features of our hands and wrists make it impossible for us to keep the clubface squared to the swing direction all the time. A golfer has to cock his wrists in the backswing and uncock them before impact to square the clubface. This action requires perfect timing and is a major cause for ball striking inconsistency.

An elbow also functions like a hinge and has a more limited range of motion. Without involving the shoulder, an elbow can only move the forearm for about 150 degrees along one axis.

With the elbow against your side, the spot where it touches on the rib cage is referred to in this book as the *elbow rest point*, which is slightly above the belt line for most people, as shown in Fig. 3-3. The elbow rest point is also above the SSP for a typical golfer.

When a golfer puts his right forearm at or near the elbow rest point level, it is very difficult for him to move the club beyond the side of his body. The restrictions from the wrists and elbows affect the way a golfer swings his club, as will be explained later.

THE SETUP

In a conventional golf swing, a golfer typically sets up to the ball with a posture demonstrated in Fig. 3-4. This style of setup has a few characteristics:

- The golfer's upper body is straight and bends forward significantly (about 40 degrees in this case) from his hips.
- The golfer's hands are relaxed and dangling straight down, nearly vertical to the ground.
- From down-the-line view, the golfer's arms and the club do not form a straight line.
- The angle between the club shaft and the golfer's upper body is close to 90 degrees.

In the conventional setup, the SSP line typically runs across the golfer's belt line and is *below* his elbow rest point. The NSP usually passes through his upper body at or near the elbow rest point.

Fig. 3-4 The Setup Shaft Plane

With the plane (SSP or NSP) running through or under the elbow rest point, the limited range of motion of the right wrist and right elbow presents a major challenge for a right-handed golfer in his effort to conduct a true one-plane full swing.

THE BACKSWING

From the setup position, the golfer would rotate his upper body and move his arms and club up and around to start the energy loading process. He would naturally tend to move the club up and around his body along the SSP, as a swing robot would do.

The golfer is able to move the club along the SSP all the way to the position where the club is parallel to the ground. After his club moves beyond this point, he will soon encounter some restrictions.

Club is parallel to ground

Fig. 3-5 The Parallel Position in Backswing

THE RIGHT WRIST AND RIGHT ELBOW

As we mentioned earlier, the SSP typically runs below the elbow rest point in a conventional setup. This interferes with the execution of a one-plane swing. Beyond the parallel position, the limited range of motion of the right wrist and right elbow will restrict club movement and prevent the club from traveling further up along the SSP because neither the elbow nor the wrist can flex sideways to let that happen. At this point, the golfer has three options:

36

1. Gives up the effort to move the club further up along the SSP and stops there to execute a quarter-swing.
2. Moves the club further up along the SSP, but has to sway his upper body to make it happen.
3. Folds the right elbow and pushes the club up above the SSP, then rotates the club further around his body.

A quarter-swing does not generate enough swing speed, and therefore is not an option in competition. Swaying the upper body dramatically would compromise ball striking consistency and is not an option either.

In order to get around the blockage from the joints and continue moving the club further up and around the body for more power, the golfer would have to give up the effort of swinging the club on one plane. He would bend his right forearm up so he can take the club further around his body. This action naturally and inevitably pushes the right hand, and consequently the club, to a position above the SSP, as show in Fig. 3-6.

Fig. 3-6 Overcoming the Elbow Blockage

Interestingly, the action that pushes the club above the SSP happens so naturally that an average golfer wouldn't even realize that his club has moved away from that plane. With his upper body tilted, the golfer's spatial perception can be a little confused and fail to notice the deviation. He would feel that he swings the club on a plane the entire time.

Since the club does not move on a plane during the entire backswing, the surface on which it travels during this stage should not be called a backswing plane. *For human golfers, there is no backswing plane in a full conventional swing.* This is also true for Ben Hogan's swing. If we study his swing video carefully, we will notice that Mr. Hogan, who was considered as having a flat swing, also pushed his club above his SSP at the top.

Nonetheless, it is possible to keep the club on plane throughout the entire backswing in certain scenarios: when the swing scale is limited, such as a quarter-swing or a short half-swing; or the player is using an unconventional setup, which will be discussed below.

THE ALTERNATIVE SETUP

Although not a popular choice, a fourth option is available for golfers willing to be unconventional and creative like Moe Norman: resorting to an alternative setup.

The Moe Norman Style

Fig. 3-7 The Alternative Setup

If a golfer sets up to the ball with the SSP running well above the elbow rest point, the right elbow and right wrist blockage will naturally be defeated. It is then possible to keep the club on the SSP throughout the entire backswing.

That is exactly what Canadian legendary golfer Moe Norman did. Moe raised his arms at setup and extended them towards the ball. So his club and his arms were on the SSP, which was raised well above the elbow rest point and passed through his shoulders.

With this setup, his right elbow and right wrist had enough room to flex and the blockage was no longer an issue.

Moe Norman didn't have to push his club higher than the SSP in the backswing most of the time, and consequently didn't have to lower it during the downswing. This is probably the only setup that allows a human golfer to execute a swing that closely resembles the robot-style swing.

However, this unique swing style has not gained popularity among golfers, possibly due to its unstylish appearance and the lack of comfort and distance.

THE DOWNSWING

In order to hit the ball on the sweet spot of the clubface, the golfer would have to swing the club down on a NSP that is reasonably close to the SSP. He simply can't set up with the club on one plane and expect to hit the ball solidly and consistently from another that is drastically different.

With the left arm raised high at the top of the backswing, the club is typically above the NSP for almost every player. Even Moe Norman often pushed his club above his striking plane.

In order to launch the ball straight toward the target, there is one important move a golfer must do at the early downswing: dropping the club onto a lower striking plane, which should be fairly close to his SSP, as soon as possible. He must accomplish this before the club enters the impact zone. Once the club is on the striking plane, he must keep it moving on that plane through impact. These are the common and fundamental features you can see in the swing of every great player.

THE KEY MOVE IN THE DOWNSWING

Every great golfer, regardless of the generation he belongs to and swing style he possesses, exhibits a key move during the early stage of his downswing. This key move is dropping the club onto the striking plane, which is ideally the NSP. This is the most important task for a golfer in the initial stage of the downswing.

This key move is in sync with the initial body actions described in Ben Hogan's *Five Lessons*. The lateral lower body movement, the weight shift, and the drop of the right shoulder all happen simultaneously to facilitate the club lowering action.

Some professional players, such as Tiger Woods, exhibit a squat-down action during the downswing to accelerate the plane alignment process, as well as to generate more power. This is probably why Tiger usually gets his club on the NSP sooner than many other players.

Fig. 3-8 The Key Move in the Downswing

A great player usually gets his club on the NSP slightly below the half-swing position and then keeps it there throughout the impact zone. A good player might find his plane a little bit later, but still before the quarter-swing position. A poor player can barely get his club on plane before entering the impact zone.

The sooner a golfer can set the club onto the NSP, the earlier he can start the acceleration fearlessly to generate more momentum.

A BEGINNER'S FIRST MOVE

As said earlier, the plane deviation during the backswing happens so naturally that an average golfer wouldn't even realize that he has moved the club above the NSP at the completion of the backswing. To him, it feels like the club has moved up along a perfect "backswing plane" the entire time.

With the club above the NSP at the top, a beginner who is unaware of the plane deviation would naturally and instinctively want to attack the ball directly via a straight line, because this is easy and comfortable to do. Without a good understanding of the swing plane and club movement, dropping the club is not part of his plan.

And here is how the trouble begins.

WHY DOES A BEGINNER SLICE?

The straight line attack from the top produces the problematic and notorious outside-in downswing move. The club's actual striking plane cuts across the NSP from outside to inside.

If a golfer has the basic knowledge of ball flight physics, he will know this outside-in downswing has a great tendency to produce a slice spin, depending on where the club is facing at impact.

This is exactly why most beginners slice their drives. How often do you see a beginner begging for a quick fix for his hook? I would say probably never.

The golfer in Fig. 3-9, Andrew Arbesfeld, can hit slice shots consistently with his driver. The pictures captured from his swing video clearly show that he was making the typical over-the-top (i.e.

outside-in) downswing move.

The dash line in the picture represents Andrew's NSP. As can be clearly seen, the club was still way above the NSP near his quarter-swing position and was not at all parallel to it. His club shaft was outside of his right shoulder. If you go back to Fig. 3-8, you will see the pro, Dan, has his club below his right shoulder at a similar swing position.

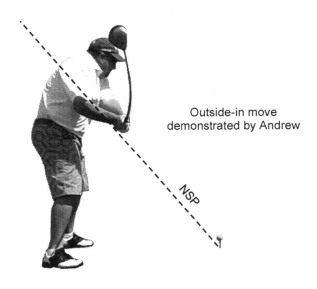

Outside-in move
demonstrated by Andrew

NSP

Fig. 3-9 The Outside-in Downswing Move

At this point, there was little chance that Andrew could get the club back on the NSP before entering the impact zone. A slice or a pull was unavoidable.

4. A Different Perspective

Why must I keep my right elbow close to my side? Why should I keep my head behind the ball? Why should I start the downswing with a lateral movement? Why…?

The list can go on forever.

The movements of the club and the body in a golf swing have always been a perplexing subject for many average golfers. The piecemeal quick fixes and tips, which have saturated the golf magazines, YouTube videos, and books, are supposed to address such issues but have often made golfers even more confused. The reasons behind these quick fixes and tips are seldom explained and golfers can rarely challenge their validity.

To answer these questions, golfers must be able to capture the big picture of a golf swing. Understanding the essence of the swing plane will be the first step.

Fortunately, our bodies and minds naturally have the ability to conduct many sophisticated tasks, including an effective golf swing. All we need to do is finding a way to release that potential.

We often see things we don't normally see by taking a different perspective. In this chapter, we will take a look at the golf swing from a more intuitive and comprehensible angle. This new perspective will go a long way in helping you better understand the golf swing. It will answer all the questions we listed in the first paragraph. More importantly, it is also a great tool for diagnosing issues in the future.

THE HUMAN PERCEPTION

The body coordination, visual perception, and spatial perception of a human being are amazingly complex and all involved in a golf swing. Before looking at the swing from a new perspective, it would be a great idea to briefly discuss the human perception.

In 1962, American psychologist Herman Witkin introduced the concept of *field dependence* after his intensive study on human cognitive styles. Through the famous *Rod and Frame Test*, in which a person is asked to adjust a rod within a tilted frame to a vertical position in a dark room, Dr. Witkin discovered that a person could be categorized as either field dependent or field independent regarding his spatial perception.

A field dependent person relies on the external cues to judge the orientation of an object and his spatial perception is affected by the tilt of the frame or the tilt of his body, whereas a field independent person disregards the external cues and uses information and sensors from his own body in making the determination.

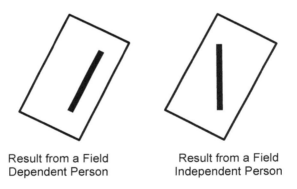

Result from a Field
Dependent Person

Result from a Field
Independent Person

Fig. 4-1 The Rod and Frame Test

Regardless of his type, a person's visual and spatial perceptions are always more accurate at the horizontal and vertical directions when his head is in a normal upright position. He can easily tell whether a line is leveled or vertical because in real world scenarios we have a lot of cues and references in these two directions and our sensors have been well trained and calibrated. For instance, the

44

surface of a lake is perfectly leveled and a string hung with a weight attached to its end is perfectly vertical.

Here is a simple experiment to quickly test your spatial perception. Find a big mirror, such as the one in your master bathroom or the wall mirror in a gym. Face the mirror, stand upright, and close your eyes. Then extend both arms on your sides to form a leveled straight line, as shown in Fig. 4-2.

Fig. 4-2 Straight Arm Test 1

When you believe both arms are on a straight line, open your eyes and check the result in the mirror. How did you do? Most likely you have done an excellent job. Congratulations!

Now let's change to a different posture. With your right side facing the mirror, take a golf setup stance with your upper body bent forward, as shown in Fig. 4-3.

Keep your left arm straight and point it to where the golf ball would be and close your eyes. Next, extend your right arm behind you and try to keep both arms on a straight line, as shown in Fig. 4-3. When you are ready, open your eyes and check the result in the mirror.

Fig. 4-3 Straight Arm Test 2

Are you able to get both arms on a straight line? If you are, congratulations again for the great job! If you are not, don't feel bad, you are not alone. Many people find it harder to keep their arms on a straight line when their heads are tilted because their ability to sense the position of the arm is compromised. It just means your perceptive sensors might need some tune-up in such a posture. Many people who initially failed the second test would pass with flying colors after some practice. That means our perceptions and sensations can be improved through training.

The second test actually has a lot to do with a golf swing. Many beginners fail to align their clubs properly to the NSP or are completely unable to move their clubs on a plane within the impact zone because their spatial perceptions could use some calibration.

When I did the second test for the first time, my right arm was too flat. With both arms on a straight line, the right arm actually felt overly steep to me. This issue might have contributed to my inside takeaway and the tendency to lay off the club during downswing in the past. The second test can indeed help a golfer do better in sensing the position and orientation of his club during a golf swing, and therefore can be a useful drill in practice sessions.

A DIFFERENT PERSPECTIVE

The challenges people are facing in learning golf could have a lot to do with the typical swing posture, in which the upper body is tilted and the club is swung on an inclined surface. Our spatial perception may not be as sharp in such a scenario as they are in a normal upright posture, at least not for everybody.

To temporarily get around this obstacle and activate our powerful intuitive potentials, we will be looking at the golf swing from a different perspective. When we swing with an upright posture, our spatial perception and sensations work the best and will give us a totally different experience.

Fig. 4-4 The Conventional Setup

Fig. 4-4 shows Dan with a conventional setup posture. The angle between his upper body and the club shaft is close to 90 degrees. If we "freeze" everything above his hips, including his arms and the club, and bend them backward from the hips until his upper body is vertical. He now sets up with an upright swing posture, similar to the one shown in Fig. 4-5.

47

THE UPRIGHT SETUP

For the upright posture, we will also move the ball to the golfer's waist level. Now his goal is to hit the ball to the left by swinging the club on a nearly horizontal plane. By taking this setup, the golfer will have a much better perception on the position and orientation of the club, as well as its course of movement. The SSP line runs through the golfer's belt line and is below his elbow rest point. His upper body may tilt to the right slightly as in a normal golf swing.

Fig. 4-5 The Upright Setup

THE UPRIGHT TAKEAWAY

In the takeaway, the golfer turns his upper body clockwise until the club points to the right. During this step, the golfer keeps his arms and the club relatively fixed to his upper body by maintaining the shoulder-arm triangle. This promotes a more powerful upper body turn. During the takeaway, the club moves along the SSP or slightly above it.

With the upright posture, it is very obvious that letting the club drop below the SSP (i.e. an inside takeaway) is a meaningless and error-prone move. Since the club will end up above the SSP at the completion of the backswing, why waste time and energy letting it go below in the first place? In addition, an inside takeaway can potentially get the club to an improper position at the top of the backswing.

Fig. 4-6 The Upright Takeaway

The change of perspective allows us to see things we don't normally see. For example, we wouldn't notice an inside takeaway and its disadvantages so easily with a conventional setup.

We can also see why moving the club up with active arms or quickly moving it too high above the SSP is also a bad idea. In either case, the body will not coil enough and the club may arrive at an undesirable position at the top.

THE UPRIGHT BACKSWING

At the completion of the takeaway, the golfer wants to continue with the body rotation and also get the club further around his torso for more power. However, the right elbow and right wrist now have difficulty moving further along the SSP due to their limited ranges of motion at the waist level. The club movement is restricted.

To continue moving the club around his body, the golfer will have to flex his right elbow, which in turn moves his right forearm

49

up. This action also conveniently gets the right wrist out of the way, but inevitably pushes the club higher above the SSP. The higher a golfer raises his arms, the easier he can get the club around his body.

With the upright swing posture, we can easily see how the club gradually moves above the SSP after the takeaway. If a golfer takes a conventional setup posture, in which his upper body bends forward, he will very likely fail to notice the club's deviation from the SSP. He would feel as if the club had moved along a "backswing plane," which doesn't actually exist, all the way to the top.

Left shoulder gets higher

Fig. 4-7 The Upright Backswing

The clubhead leads the way in the upswing and would naturally point upward, thus the club is normally steeper than the SSP. It is also acceptable to have the club parallel to the SSP, but obviously there is no reason to lay it off by pointing the clubhead toward the ground. We should also notice that the left shoulder is getting higher than the right one in the process.

THE UPRIGHT BACKSWING TOP

The golfer continues to move his hands higher as he keeps moving the club around his body. His hands are approximately at his left shoulder level when he finishes the backswing. Some golfers' hands are higher than others at this point, depending on their individual

50

swing styles. Tiger Woods' hands are usually much higher than Matt Kuchar's at this position.

With the upright posture, we can also see something interesting at the top of the backswing: the golfer's left shoulder is much higher than the right one. *The shoulder line is tilted and not perpendicular to the spine* due to the anatomical structure of the shoulder joints. The shoulders are leveled at setup, but as the left arm moves higher after the takeaway, the left shoulder is raised to a higher position and the shoulder line inclines.

What does this mean? It tells us the shoulders do not move on a plane in a golf swing. The "shoulder plane" we often hear of does not exist either.

Fig. 4-8 The Upright Top

If you have a tendency to sway your hips to the right side during the backswing, you can now easily understand why it is not a good idea. With your upper body leaning to the left due to hip swaying, it is more difficult to bring the club to the NSP during the downswing since your hips must travel extra distance during the lateral movement to shift the weight to your left foot.

The Upright Downswing

With the backswing completed, the golfer is now ready to transition into the most important stage: the downswing, where the uncoiling and the ball striking are executed.

But wait a second, there is a problem here. The club is now at the golfer's shoulder level, yet the ball is down at his waist level. The golfer's instinct will tell him to attack the ball directly via a straight route pointing to the ground, just like chopping down a tree. If his job is to simply smash the ball then this move is perfectly fine. However, the goal here is to hit the ball to the left. The straight line attack is going to be disastrous because it will either knock the ball to the ground or produce a slice spin as the club cuts across the ball.

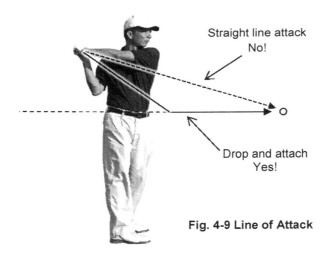

Fig. 4-9 Line of Attack

To launch the ball as intended, the golfer will have to swing the club on a striking plane that runs along the target line.

Since the golfer sets up to the ball with a nearly horizontal SSP at his waist level, the striking plane must be reasonably close to it so he can return the sweet spot of the clubface behind the ball. Therefore, the club must first be dropped to a lower striking plane, and then be released on that plane to hit the ball. Actually, a baseball swing also features a similar dropping action.

Some readers might have a question here. Why couldn't the golfer, from the top of swing, simply swing the club on a steeper striking plane (the "shoulder plane") that runs along the target line? Then he wouldn't have to first drop the club to a lower plane.

This is a great question! Let's check it out. In a conventional setup, the club and left arm are not on a straight line. The left shoulder, hands, and clubhead define a triangle, as shown in Fig. 4-10. According to the geometry we learned at school, the total length of the left arm (A) and the club (B) is greater than the distance from the left shoulder to the ball (C) in this triangle.

If the club travels on this much steeper striking plane, then at impact the left arm and the club are almost on a straight line. Their total length is longer than the distance from the left shoulder to the ball. Unless the golfer changes his posture drastically to absorb the slack (the extra length), the clubhead at impact will fail to return to its setup position and will either shank or completely miss the ball.

Since at impact the golfer's body is open to the target and his left shoulder moves away from its position at setup, some slack is taken away and the NSP is usually a few degrees steeper than the SSP. However, in no case can it be 15 degrees steeper, unless the golfer stands up at impact to absorb the slack.

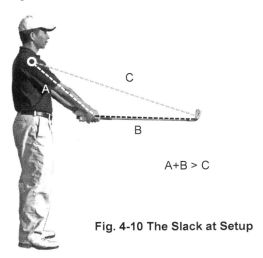

A+B > C

Fig. 4-10 The Slack at Setup

As a general rule, the NSP must be reasonably close to the SSP in order to deliver a consistent and solid impact, hence the necessity to drop the club to a lower striking plane during the downswing.

THE KEY MOVE

With the help of the new perspective, we can see that one of the primary tasks in the early downswing is to drop the club onto a lower striking plane.

With the upright posture, many people will instinctively know what to do without taking any expensive lessons because they can clearly see where the club is now, where it needs to go, and what must be done.

With his hands and club at his shoulder level, the golfer will naturally execute three actions simultaneously to drop the club to a lower NSP in order to hit the ball at the waist level.

- Sliding his hips left & keeping his head behind the ball.
- Lowering his right shoulder with right elbow close to side.
- Raising his left shoulder.

While sliding his hips to the left, the golfer makes room for the club to drop. He will also naturally keep his head at its original position to facilitate this process. It is more difficult to lower the club if the head moves along with the weight shift. You will notice these moves can be done more easily if the upper body leans slightly to the right at setup.

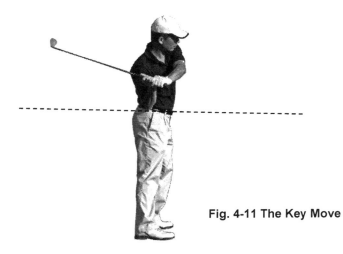

Fig. 4-11 The Key Move

54

As the shoulders change positions, the golfer's spine inevitably tilts toward the right to help the club get on the NSP. Obviously, the spine angle does not stay constant in a golf swing. As the right shoulder drops, the right elbow naturally sticks to the side of the body to help lower the club.

At this stage, the golfer should keep his hands passive and maintain the wrist cock so the club is not released prematurely. Early release will not only result in poor swing speed, but also interfere with the club alignment process. This is similar to what we see in a baseball swing.

The club should move at a relatively low speed during the plane alignment stage. Only after getting on the NSP can it be accelerated and released vigorously to strike the ball.

THE UPRIGHT NSP

Once the club gets on the NSP, the golfer can start accelerating the club through active body rotation, and then release it to deliver a powerful strike. The NSP can be the same as the SSP or slightly steeper.

Fig. 4-12 Get Back on Plane

Here the club enters the high-speed impact zone, where it is extremely important for the club to swing on plane the entire time to produce predictable and solid shots.

The Upright Impact

At impact, the golfer squares the clubface to the target line. After hitting the ball, he would naturally cross his forearms. His right forearm will come over the left one in an effort to keep the club on plane and absorb the residual energy safely.

The golfer instinctively engages his lower body to create more power. At impact, he would naturally have his body open to the target and his hands ahead of the ball.

During the follow through, the club will continue moving due to its residual momentum and again rise above the NSP due to the left elbow blockage.

Fig. 4-13 The Upright Impact

Another Way to Get around the Blockage

We have previously talked about getting around the anatomical restrictions by raising the NSP above the elbow rest point. This approach can also be better understood from the new perspective.

With the upright swing position, if the ball is placed at shoulder level and the golfer sets up with his arms extended to the ball, then the SSP is well above the elbow rest point as a horizontal plane passing through his shoulders.

In this case, the right elbow and wrist are no longer blocking the club rotation along the SSP and the club can now move on the same plane throughout the entire backswing.

During the downswing, there is no need for the club to switch to a different plane either. The club never leaves the SSP and is on the perfect position to strike. Just let the club stay on the same plane to finish the job. Moving it higher or lower than the SSP would feel awkward.

This setup, as shown in Fig. 4-14, is in fact the robot-style one-plane swing executed by a human with the upright posture.

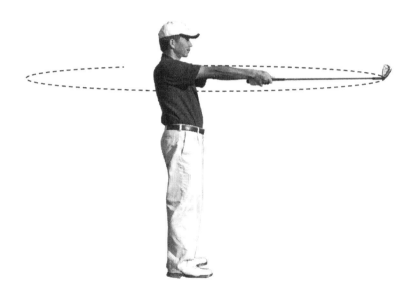

Fig. 4-14 The Upright One-Plane Setup

Please bear in mind that with this setup there is no slack between the left shoulder and the ball. The golfer would risk missing the ball if he opens his body too aggressively at impact, unless he makes extra adjustments to his posture. Consequently this setup might feel a little tense and awkward.

Summary

In the upright posture swing, a golfer put his head to the normal upright position in which his spatial perception works the best. He can then clearly see things that are less obvious in a regular golf posture and transfer the knowledge learned to an actual golf swing.

The upright posture swing can help a golfer better understand the fundamentals of the swing, learn the correct movements, and troubleshoot confusing issues. It is a very effective learning tool. Based on my personal experience, I would even call it my virtual self-learning school. It has answered many questions and cleared a lot of confusion for me.

Whenever you have questions or feel puzzled in the future, try going back to the upright posture to seek answers and inspiration. Very likely your will find what you need here.

5. THE STRIKING PLANE SWING MODEL

Having learned the swing with the upright posture, it is much easier to understand the proper sequence of a normal golf swing.

Essentially, the movement in a conventional golf swing is the same as that with the upright posture; the main difference is the upper body tilt angle.

From the upright posture, a golfer gets back to the conventional golf setup by bending his upper body forward from the hips and flexing his knees. He can then transfer all the things learned over to the normal golf swing.

In this chapter, we will summarize and explain the principles of swing movement in a conventional golf swing and systematically present them as the *Striking Plane Swing Model*. The word *model* simply means a framework of essential information. The model itself is very simple and no math is involved. As a road map for club movement, it will be an effective tool in your journey to a better game.

THE PRINCIPLES OF THE STRIKING PLANE SWING MODEL

The Striking Plane Swing Model is extracted from the swings of numerous great players. It is supported by the principles of classical mechanics and the knowledge of human anatomy. The following are the fundamental principles that the model is established upon.

Principle 1: Within the impact zone, the *entire* golf club must travel on a *plane* to deliver predictable, stable, and consistent shots.

Principle 2: To produce the maximum possible clubhead speed and align with the striking plane properly, the club should be released within a compact striking slot.

Principle 3: In a conventional full swing, a golfer is not able to swing the club on one plane throughout the entire backswing because of his anatomical limitations. The club will move above the NSP at the top of the backswing.

Principle 4: In a conventional full swing, a golfer is not able to swing the club on one plane throughout the entire downswing due to alignment and consistency reasons. To make solid contact, the club must be dropped to a lower NSP, which should be fairly close to the SSP, before entering the high speed impact zone.

Principle 1 is the foundation of the model, as well as the key feature of a consistent golf swing. It is supported by the theory of physics, particularly classical mechanics.

The predictability is based on the following fact: the velocity of an object moving in a circular motion always points along the tangent direction of the arc. As long as the striking plane meets the ground along the target line, the clubhead velocity at the bottom of the swing arc always points straight to the target, regardless of the inclination angle of the plane.

The stability is the result of keeping the club shaft on plane within the impact zone, so the torque of a head-on impact won't knock the clubhead out of the striking plane (see chapter one).

Principle 2 might not appear to have a direct connection with the swing plane, but it actually affects plane alignment during the downswing and is also a key characteristic of a high quality swing. The same amount of club shaft angular movement (about 90 degrees from parallel-to-ground to impact,) released over a shorter interval will produce greater acceleration and can therefore result in higher clubhead speed at impact. In a compact release, the clubhead will also travel along an arc of a smaller radius, which means better ground clearance before impact.

A club released over a longer interval will fail to achieve its maximum possible speed. The clubhead is also more likely to touch the ground before impact due to its greater swing radius and shallower angle of attack.

Principles 3 and 4 have been explained thoroughly in the previous chapters. They are the physical limitations that a golfer must be fully aware of in order to execute a conventional swing with the proper sequence.

In the following sections, we will go over every step of a golf swing and explain the swing model in detail.

THE SETUP

The main purpose of setup is to find a position that allows the golfer to return his clubhead precisely behind the ball *at impact*. To accomplish this goal, the golfer doesn't necessarily set up with the center of his clubface behind the ball. For example, Zach Johnson sets up with the toe of his clubhead behind the ball. As another example, Moe Norman sets up with his clubhead about 12 inches away behind the ball. So, it is acceptable to adjust the clubhead position at setup to achieve the best outcome at impact, as long as it delivers consistent results.

There are at least two ways to set up to a ball in a golf swing: the *conventional setup* and the *one-plane setup*.

In the conventional setup, which is the mainstream style among tour players, the golfer bends his upper body forward from the hips significantly. His arms are relaxed and point nearly straight down for mid and short irons, but may extend slightly toward the target line for fairway woods and drivers. His upper body and the club shaft form an angle that is very close to 90 degrees. With such a setup, the SSP typically passes through the golfer's belt line and is *below* his right elbow rest point, as shown in Fig. 5-1.

Fig. 5-1 The Conventional Setup

Fig. 5-2 The One-Plane Setup

In the one-plane setup, the golfer bends his upper body forward from the hips. His arms extend to the ball and form a straight line with the club shaft (Fig. 5-2). The SSP extends through the golfer's shoulder joints or the armpits and is *above* his right elbow rest point.

With either style, the golfer's upper body tilts right slightly as the left hand is higher on the shaft. The tilted body also makes the downswing moves easier, as discussed in chapter four.

Most modern professional players use the conventional setup, which appears to be more natural, elegant, relaxing, and comfortable, but might be less straightforward in execution to beginners. This setup style also allows a golfer to keep his wrists at a more stable angle to embrace the force at impact. Considering all these, our discussions of the Striking Plane Swing Model will focus on the conventional swing.

The Benefit of the 90-degree Angle

You might have wondered why a professional player usually sets up with a nearly 90-degree angle between his upper body and the club. Actually, there is a good reason for it from a technical point of view.

Within the impact zone, the club swings around the golfer's torso, which is also rotating. The combined motion makes it a tricky business to keep the club moving on plane. Getting the striking plane perpendicular to the upper body makes keeping the club moving on plane easier. With such a setup, the body and the club rotate in sync around the same axis and the body rotation does not affect the club swing plane.

On the other hand, if the striking plane is not perpendicular to the body, the body rotation will drag the club shaft away from the plane it is on. This issue can be more serious in a professional level swing, where the body rotation is fast and aggressive. If the club shaft is not perpendicular to the body rotational axis, it can be taken along a curved surface by the body (as seen in Fig 2-2). Although a golfer can make dynamic compensations to keep the club on plane, but that will be a very difficult thing to do.

If the club is not moving on a plane within the impact zone, ball striking quality can be compromised. This is why it is a good idea to keep the angle between the club and torso close to 90 degrees.

THE TAKEAWAY

During the takeaway, the golfer rotates his upper body clockwise from the setup position until the club is parallel to the ground and pointing to the right. Early in this step, the golfer keeps his arms and the club passive and relatively fixed to his upper body by maintaining the triangle formed by his chest and arms. This one-piece takeaway promotes better upper body rotation for a more powerful coil. A takeaway dominated by active arm movement weakens the body rotation, and therefore is undesirable.

The club should ideally move up along the space between the SSP and the NSP during the takeaway. Tiger Woods keeps his hands on the SSP while moving the clubhead along the NSP in many of his swings. However, a takeaway is acceptable as long as the club is reasonably close to the SSP or NSP, since eventually the club will move above both planes.

Fig. 5-3 Takeaway

An inside takeaway, which means the club drops noticeably below the SSP, is not recommended because it involves unnecessary detour and rerouting. It can also easily lead to an undesirable club position at the top and cause problems in the downswing. However, this is not to say an inside takeaway will definitely cause trouble. Some great players take their clubs away along an inside path, yet they all quickly lift the clubs above the SSP beyond the half-swing position. Nancy Lopez, who won 48 LPGA tour events in her professional career, is a perfect example. An inside takeaway requires good body coordination and accurate spatial perception, and therefore is not a recommended style for average golfers.

The other extreme, which is picking up the club in front of the body or moving the club above the SSP too fast, can also be problematic. This type of move is very common among beginners because it feels natural and comfortable. A takeaway like this usually leads to an incorrect club position at the top and insufficient body rotation.

Without sufficient shoulder turn on the top, the club doesn't have enough room to drop onto the NSP in time. This can easily result in the notorious outside-in downswing and is a major cause for slices.

Keeping the clubhead close to the ground and moving it along the target line for the first 12-24 inches is a good way to avoid an inside takeaway.

THE PARALLEL POSITION

At the completion of the takeaway, the club reaches the hip level and is parallel to the ground. This is a good checkpoint for club position.

Ideally, the hands and club should be on or slightly above the SSP. The club is parallel to the ground and points straight to the right. Some modern tour players may have their clubs above the SSP and pointing slightly outside the plane, but very few of them have the clubs under the SSP and pointing to the back. Some older generation golfers, such as Arnold Palmer, do point their clubs to the back, but they could also quickly correct it as the club moved to the top.

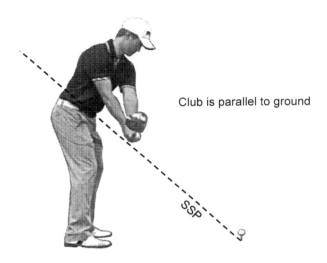

Club is parallel to ground

SSP

Fig. 5-4 Backswing Parallel Position

Beyond this point, the right elbow and the right wrist will soon get in the way and make it very difficult to for the club to continue moving along the SSP or NSP.

THE HALF-SWING POSITION

After the completion of takeaway, the golfer wishes to continue moving the club up and around along the SSP for stronger coiling, but now his right elbow and right wrist get in the way and prevent the club from moving along the plane further.

Left arm is parallel to ground

Fig. 5-5 Halfway in Backswing

To overcome the blockage and give room for the right elbow to flex, the golfer gradually pushes the club above the SSP.

When the golfer reaches the half-swing position, which is another important checkpoint, his left arm is parallel to the ground and his hands and club are already above the SSP.

At this position, the club shaft may or may not be parallel to the SSP. Since the club is in a process of moving up and the clubhead leads the way, it is quite natural and common to see the shaft being steeper than the SSP. However, it is undesirable to set the club flatter than the SSP, as will be explained later.

At the half-swing position, you may observe a significant difference on the extent of left wrist cocking among different players. Many good professional players' left wrists are not yet fully cocked at this point; the angle between their left arms and the clubs is greater than 90 degrees. As a comparison, an amateur player might have a tendency to over-cock his left wrist at this point and the angle between his left arm and shaft is smaller than 90 degrees.

Fig. 5-6 A Pro's Delayed Wrist Cock Halfway at Backswing

To a golfer's mind, a fully cocked left wrist can be a signal indicating a finishing backswing and may cause the body to stop rotating prematurely. In this sense, delaying the full left wrist cock can promote a more powerful shoulder turn.

THE CLUB ORIENTATION AT BACKSWING

There are conflicting opinions on where the end of the club should point to as it travels above the waist level in the backswing. Here are some typical opinions you might have come across in various publications.

- The club end should always point to the target line unless it is parallel to it.
- The club end should point inside the target line, but no closer to the golfer than the middle point between his feet line and target line. The end of the club and this zone form the so-called golden triangle.
- The club should be parallel to the SSP and its end should point outside the target line.

This is quite confusing. What should we choose to follow? Now that we have learned the principles of club movement in a golf swing, this can be understood more easily.

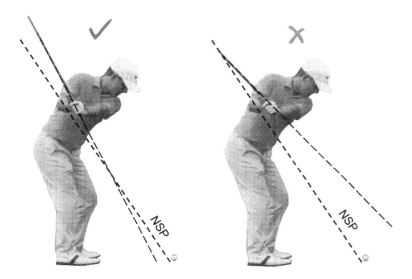

Maintain a zero or positive angle to the NSP

Fig. 5-7 Club Orientation in Backswing

Ideally, we want to keep the club shaft parallel to the NSP. This makes it easy to set the club to a proper position at the top and will make things much easier during the downswing. In this case, the club end should point to somewhere not too far outside the target line.

In an actual backswing, when the club starts to go above the SSP or the NSP at the half-swing position, the clubhead usually leads the way and rises earlier than the hands. Consequently, the club would commonly be set at a steeper angle than the NSP at this point and the club end will point to the target line, or slightly inside.

The club should not be any flatter than the SSP; otherwise the golfer must work against gravity to set the club to a proper top position. This adjustment can be error-prone and uncomfortable.

As the club moves higher than the half position in the backswing, it gets further above the NSP and tends to be parallel to it.

Some players' clubs may start pointing slightly outside the target line near the top.

What really matters here is not where the end of the club points to, it is the angle between the club and the NSP. It is not desirable to set the shaft flatter than the NSP. The angle between them should be zero or positive.

THE TOP OF BACKSWING

To execute a full swing, the golfer continues to turn his shoulders and the club. He also raises the club higher. Regardless of swing styles, all players using the conventional setup push their clubs above the NSP at the top of a full swing. Moe Norman was often able to keep his club on the NSP during the entire backswing because he used an unconventional setup, which allowed him to avoid the elbow blockage.

Left arm is high above
the SSP & NSP

Fig. 5-8 Top of the Backswing

The upper backswing is the stage which dominates a viewer's impression on a swing because the motion here is relatively slow and can be seen and remembered well. Therefore, this is typically the stage where different swing styles are perceived and defined.

Players, such as Ben Hogan and Matt Kuchar, keep their clubs close to the NSP, possibly with the intention to drop them onto the NSP quicker. At the top of the backswing, Matt's left arm is nearly parallel to his shoulder line. Hogan's left arm is a little steeper. That is why their swings appear to be flat. These two players are also considered by many as the "one-plane" swingers according to Jim Hardy's definition.

Fig. 5-9 Steep vs. Flat

Tiger Woods and most other modern professional players choose to push their arms and clubs much higher above the NSP for more power. Tiger's left forearm is usually much steeper than his shoulder line at the top. Jim Furyk, Dustin Johnson, and Bubba Watson all have their leading arms pointing to the sky.

These players' arms are set at very steep angles at the top and therefore give people the impression that they also strike the balls on very steep NSPs. However, video analyses revealed this is not the case at all. The two players shown in Fig 5-9 appear to have drastically different swing planes. Yet the striking planes their clubs move on in the lower half of the downswing are both inclined at 50 degrees! *They both have the same swing plane!*

71

THE RANGE OF PLANE DEVIATION

In this book, we will use *range of plane deviation* or simply *range* to describe a unique parameter at the top of the backswing: the distance between the golfer's hands and the NSP.

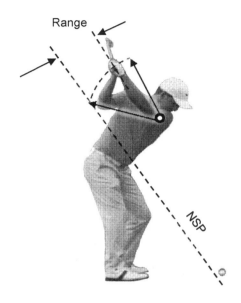

Fig. 5-10 Range of Plane Deviation

Range affects the appearance of a swing and is one of the key elements for swing style. It can also affect ball striking power and downswing timing.

Since the left arm moves around the left shoulder joint, range also affects the hand position on both vertical and horizontal directions. When the hands are raised higher, they are also closer to the front of the body. With the hands positioned lower, they are closer to the back. The hand position will influence the initial move in the downswing.

A golfer with a greater range will rely more on vertical drop and less on body rotation to bring his club down to the NSP, whereas one with smaller range will rely more on body rotation to bring the club back on plane since the club is further behind the body to begin with.

72

In chapter seven, Swing Analysis Examples, the swing of pro A, who is deemed to have a "steep plane," was compared with that of pro B, who is considered to have a "flat" swing. What was observed is quite shocking: the only major difference between their swings is the range of plane deviation. Their SSPs, NSPs, as well as their movement within the impact zone, are nearly identical. Pro A, who has a greater range, actually gets his club on the NSP earlier.

THE ROLE OF THE BACKSWING

A properly executed backswing is a beneficial element of a sound golf swing. It promotes strong body coil and allows the golfer to set the club to an ideal position at the top. All these in turn facilitate the execution of a flawless downswing.

However, a textbook backswing is not an indispensable requirement of a good golf swing. Deviation from a preferred backswing route does not necessarily lead to bad results. In theory, the path a club takes during the backswing should not have any significant influence on the quality of a shot. As long as the golfer's body is sufficiently coiled and the club and arms are properly positioned at the start of the downswing, a golfer will have every chance to hit a solid shot. This is exactly why Jack Nicklaus, Jim Furyk, and Nance Lopez played great games in spite of their unique backswing styles.

Nonetheless, this is not to discredit the positive influence of a good backswing. It is definitely a wise choice for most golfers to learn and carry out the backswing in the preferred form, which will give them better chances to hit good shots consistently.

THE DOWNSWING

The downswing is the stage where the club accumulates momentum, finds its proper alignment, and strikes the ball forcefully.

The downswing is the spirit of a golf swing. The ball striking quality is ultimately determined by what a golfer does in the stage. Even with his unusual backswing, Jim Furyk can still deliver great shots because he performs the right downswing moves.

Regardless of their backswing styles, all great players share a consistent, technically sound, and similarly looking downswing.

With the club above the NSP at the top of the backswing, a golfer's primary task in the early stage of the downswing is to *drop the club onto an appropriate striking plane,* which should ideally be the NSP for a straight shot.

In order for a club to make solid contact with the ball, the NSP shall be reasonably close to the SSP. Although both planes are nearly identical for some players, the NSP is typically a little steeper (4~7 degrees steeper for most professional players) because at impact the left shoulder has moved away from its setup position. Consequently, the club has to be moved to a steeper striking plane to compensate the change of posture.

In order to launch a ball straight toward the target consistently, the golfer will have to get the club on the NSP as soon as possible during the early stage of downswing, and then keep it precisely on that plane all the way through impact. This is the key feature that is exhibited in the swings of every great golfer.

A golfer not moving his club on plane within the impact zone may still hit good shots occasionally, but will in no way be able to do it consistently.

THE KEY MOVE IN EARLY DOWNSWING

The key move in the early downswing is to *lower the club toward the NSP.* This is the move that differentiates a seasoned player from a beginner. The sooner a golfer can drop his club onto the NSP, the earlier he can start acceleration to generate high clubhead speed. Premature acceleration may not allow enough time for the club to get on the NSP and can cause poor plane alignment. This is probably why an easier swing is more likely to produce better result for many people.

According to what we have learned from the upright swing position, the golfer will execute the following actions to lower his club:

- Sliding his hips left & keeping his head behind the ball.
- Lowering his right shoulder with right elbow close to side.
- Raising his left shoulder.

If a golfer visualizes the NSP and focuses on lowering the club to this imaginary plane, these actions can be carried out automatically and simultaneously. His right elbow will naturally stay close to his right side.

Club drops toward the NSP

Fig. 5-11 The Key Move in Early Downswing

In the meantime, the golfer shall maintain the wrist cock so the club is not released prematurely. Early release will not only result in poor clubhead speed, but also compromise club alignment. Once the club is deployed and starts moving at very high speed, it is much more difficult to adjust its position to get it on the NSP.

This key move in early downswing may feel unnatural for many beginners. The pump drill in chapter nine can help you get familiar with the proper movement.

THE CLUB ORIENTATION IN EARLY DOWNSWING

In the first half of the downswing, it is beneficial to keep the club shaft parallel to the NSP while it is moving toward the plane. This makes the alignment process much easier since the golfer only needs to move the club toward the plane. He doesn't have to adjust the shaft's angle of inclination in the meantime. Most modern tour players drop their clubs to the NSP in this fashion.

Club stays parallel to the NSP

Fig. 5-12 Club Orientation in Downswing

For players with good body coordination, the shaft can be slightly steeper (or flatter in rare cases) than the NSP in the early downswing. For instance, Sergio Garcia swings down with his club relatively flatter than his NSP, and gets the club on NSP a little later compared to many other players because he must work against the gravity to bring the club back to the proper angle. Ben Hogan also laid off his club slightly at the beginning of his downswing.

76

GETTING ONTO THE NSP

The golfer should have successfully dropped his club onto the striking plane around the quarter-swing position. From this point on, the club shall stay on this plane throughout the impact zone. The striking plane should be identical to the NSP for a pure straight shot.

Swinging the club on plane inside the impact zone is a crucial requirement for ball striking stability and consistency, as explained earlier. If a golfer is unable to keep the club on plane within the impact zone, then he may have random misses and his ball striking won't be consistent.

Fig. 5-13 Getting the Club onto the NSP

It is advantageous to be able to get the club on plane early. The earlier a golfer can get his club onto the striking plane during the downswing, the sooner he can accumulate clubhead momentum through fearless acceleration. In addition, he can be more consistent in ball striking since he would not have to rely on last moment plane alignment, especially when he is under tremendous pressure.

Most good players get the club on plane near the quarter-swing position. Some great players find the plane around the half-swing position.

In order to hit a predictable shot, a golfer must get his club on plane before it enters the impact zone, where it accelerates and releases.

Hitting from Inside?

A lot of articles and instructors teach golfers to hit the ball from inside. For example, one article, which was written by a certified instructor and published on a high profile website, claimed that the proper swing path should be "from the inside to square at impact, and then back to the inside after impact." Depending on what he meant by "inside," this piece of advice can be misleading or completely wrong.

In order to hit a straight and pure shot, a golfer must always keep the club moving on the NSP within the impact zone. The only time he should strike the ball from the inside is when he plans to hit a draw (a shot that curves to left) or a push shot (a shot that goes straight to the right side of the target).

ENTERING THE STRIKING SLOT

Once the club is on the NSP, the golfer continues to rotate his lower body and move the club along the plane for acceleration.

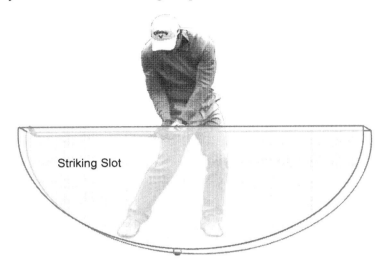

Striking Slot

Fig. 5-14   Entering the Striking Slot

When the club becomes parallel to the ground again, it is at the top edge of the impact zone and the entrance to an imaginary channel, which we call the *Striking Slot* in this book.

The striking slot is a half-moon shape channel between two imaginary parallel walls, which enclose the striking plane as the center layer. The entrance to the striking slot for a professional golfer is usually at his upper thigh level, as shown in Fig. 5-14.

The striking slot is a concept that can be used to judge the quality of release in a golf swing. It emphasizes the importance of maintaining the lag and wrist cock before entering the impact zone so the club can be released within a short duration to produce maximum acceleration.

Right at the entrance to the striking slot, the golfer should still maintain a large portion of the 90-degree angle between his left arm and the club in order to achieve the maximum clubhead speed he can potentially produce. Every great player exhibits this distinguishing feature in his full swing.

Fig. 5-15 The Striking Slot (side view)

Striking Slot

A mental image of the striking slot will help a golfer maintain his lag. He must maintain the lag to enter the striking slot cleanly because a club released prematurely will "smash" the right edge of this imaginary slot.

A professional player's striking slot is more compact than an amateur's. This can be verified by tracing the movement of his clubhead in the downswing. A wide arc here is not desired. For a typical amateur golfer, his actual striking slot is much wider and taller because he tends to release the club much earlier when it is still at his waist level (Fig. 5-16A). This means his club release process is spread across a longer time span, instead of bursting out within a shorter interval. When the same amount of inertia and angular movement (from the parallel-to-ground position to impact) are spread over a longer duration, the acceleration (and consequently the clubhead speed) he can achieve is reduced.

Since an average golfer typically starts releasing the club very early, the club will already point down to the ground as his hands reach his upper right thigh (Fig. 5-17A). A professional player or a low handicapper still maintains a large portion of his lag at the same position, as demonstrated by scratch golfer Sean Dunn in Fig. 5-17B. If an amateur who releases his club early is trying to enter a professional's striking slot, his club will for sure shatter the right edge of the channel.

With his hands still at waist level, the amateur's club is already parallel to the ground and he has lost much of his lag.

Fig. 5-16A An Amateur's Position at Downswing

At a similar arm position, a good player's club is still pointing to the sky and his lag is still intact, as demonstrated by golfer Sean Dunn.

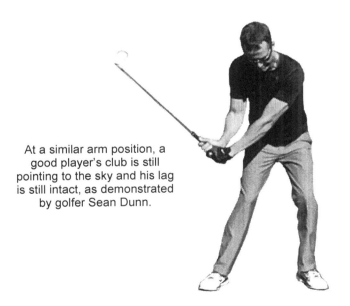

Fig. 5-16B A Good Player's Position at Downswing

With his hands over his right
thigh, the amateur's club is
already pointing to the ground.
His lag is almost gone.

Fig. 5-17A   An Amateur's Position at Downswing

At a similar arm position, a
good player still maintains most
of his lag, as demonstrated by
golfer Sean Dunn

Fig. 5-17B   A Good Player's Position at Downswing

RELEASING THE CLUB

Once inside the striking slot, the hands and wrists receive the signal to release. The golfer will then start to uncock his wrists and rotate his arms to let go the power he has accumulated. The clubhead inertia, which has been previously held by the cocked wrists, is set free to produce clubhead acceleration, to which the actions of the torso, arms, and wrists also contribute.

There's No Such Thing as a Centrifugal Force!

Many instructors in the golf community frequently credit the centrifugal force as the power source for the clubhead acceleration during release. This is technically incorrect. According to the theory of physics, *a centrifugal force does not exist*. There is no centrifugal force pulling the clubhead during a golf swing. The centrifugal *effect* we feel in a golf swing or see in a rotating washer is in fact caused by the inertia of a moving object.

According to Newton's First Law of Motion, an object is "lazy" and tends to stay at its current state unless acted upon by an external force. For instance, when a car makes a sharp turn, a passenger would feel as if a force is trying to pull him out. He looks around but couldn't find the source of such a "force." What actually happens is that his inertia is trying to keep him moving along the original direction of travel as the car turns. The seat and safety belt force him to change direction and put pressure on his body. However, the passenger feels as if the pressure is produced by a "centrifugal force."

Similarly, the clubhead would have moved on a straight line if it wasn't forced to move along a small arc by the cocked wrists. When the wrists relax and let go the 90-degree angle, the inertia of the clubhead drags the club to the release position with an angular acceleration (as the clubhead changes to a larger arc). Additional acceleration is also produced by the body rotation and the action of the hands. Please be aware, the wrist cock has another role. It allows the hands to actively accelerate the clubhead even when there is no inertia,

Nonetheless, a force, which is called the *reactive centrifugal force,* does exist according to the Newton's Third Law of Motion. This is the force the clubhead exerts back on the shaft to counter the centripetal force from the shaft. But this is not the "centrifugal force" people usually talk about, and it won't cause its own source, the clubhead, to accelerate. Just like you cannot pull yourself up in the air by dragging your own hair.

THE IMPACT

As the golfer uncocks his wrists and rotates his arms to release the club, the clubhead is returned behind the ball with its face square to the target line. Ideally, the sweet spot of the clubface is right against the ball. The quality of a shot is determined by several factors, including:

- Point of impact
- Clubhead velocity
- Clubface orientation

Point of Impact

The point of impact is an extremely important factor that is often neglected by many golfers. To achieve the maximum possible ball speed, a golfer must strike the ball on the sweet spot of the clubface. In plain language, this is called a solid contact.

A solid contact allows maximum momentum transfer from the clubhead to the ball. With everything else the same, missing the sweet spot can easily reduce the ball launch speed by 10~20%, depending on the direction and distance of the miss.

For an impact away from the sweet spot, the impact torque on the clubhead can also momentarily alter the clubface orientation and may affect the initial launch direction of the ball. For a driver or a fairway wood, a side spin will also be produced due to the gear effect and will change the ball flight shape.

Even with a perfect swing plane and flawless swing motion, a golfer must also be able to make solid contact consistently to be a good ball striker.

84

Fig. 5-18 Impact

Clubhead Velocity

Clubhead velocity represents both the speed and moving direction of the clubhead.

The magnitude of the velocity, i.e. the speed, is how fast a clubhead is moving. The greater the clubhead speed, the greater the achievable ball speed. The moving direction of clubhead can affect the launch speed, launch angle, and the spin rate of the golf ball.

Clubface Orientation

Clubface orientation refers to the angle between the clubface and the clubhead swing direction.

Clubface orientation on the vertical plane is determined by the effective loft (angle between the clubface normal and the ground) and the angle of attack (angle between clubhead moving direction and the ground), as shown in Fig. 5-19. It affects initial launch angle, launch speed, and backspin rate.

85

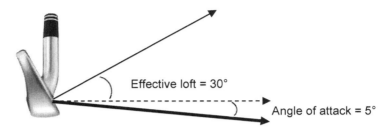

Effective loft = 30°

Angle of attack = 5°

Vertical clubface orientation is 35°

Fig. 5-19 Vertical Clubface Orientation

Given the same club and clubhead speed, the backspin is determined by the vertical clubface orientation. Leaning the club shaft forward at impact reduces the effective loft but does not necessarily change the backspin rate, which is also affected by the angle of attack. If a club leans forward five degrees and also hits down five degrees, the effective loft is reduced but the vertical orientation stays the same, so does the backspin rate.

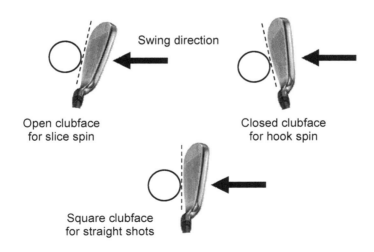

Swing direction

Open clubface
for slice spin

Closed clubface
for hook spin

Square clubface
for straight shots

Fig. 5-20 Horizontal Clubface Orientation

Clubface orientation on the horizontal plane is the angle between the horizontal grooves (or lines for drivers) and the swing direction (Fig. 5-20). It affects launch direction, launch speed, and sidespin. To hit a straight shot, a golfer must keep the clubface square to the swing direction at impact. Club orientation on the horizontal plane can be square, closed, or open, and is determined with reference to the *swing direction*, not the target line.

POST IMPACT

After the ball bounces off the clubface, how the club moves will no longer have any influence on the ball flight. However, club movement immediately after impact cannot be isolated from, instead it is closely related to, the club movement right before impact.

For a pure on-plane strike, the club will still travel on the NSP moments after impact, as shown in Fig. 5-21. This guarantees that the clubhead moving direction at the bottom of the swing arc points straight to the target.

Shaft is still on
plane after impact

Fig. 5-21   Post Impact

The club still retains a large amount of momentum after impact and cannot be stopped abruptly without causing damage. To absorb this residual energy, the arms must continue moving with the club. To keep the club moving on plane with enough extension, the arms will stay straight and cross over after impact. Arm crossover also facilitates the clubface squaring action during release.

A professional player's arms cross over very soon after impact, whereas a beginner might have a much delayed crossover or none at all. A delayed arm crossover could be the indication of a slightly open clubface at impact.

Chicken Wing

A golfer who has no arm crossover at all will often exhibit the so-called "chicken wing" arm shape after hitting the ball, as shown in Fig. 5-22. That means the golfer's left arm does not stay straight during the follow-through. Instead, the left elbow flexes to absorb the residual energy.

Fig. 5-22 Chicken Wing

The amateur golfer in the picture had no arm crossover after impact and exhibited the early stage "chicken wing." An average person cannot always see the "chicken wing" with his naked eyes, but a swing video will reveal it without mercy. Since the "chicken wing" arm shape can hurt, a golfer may unconsciously reduce the swing speed to avoid injury, and hence lose distance.

THE TWO STAGES IN DOWNSWING

The club movement in a full-scale downswing is a two-stage process. The club is above the NSP in the upper half of the downswing. It moves at a relatively low speed in order to find the proper alignment and get onto the NSP. It should achieve this goal before entering the striking slot, the earlier the better.

In the lower half of the downswing, the club stays on and moves along the striking plane to release, accelerate, and strike the ball. Since it is already on plane, the club can be swung at a much higher speed in this stage to get more distance.

Fig. 5-23 The Two Stages in the Downswing

Normally, the point where the club is parallel to the ground separates the two stages in the downswing, as shown in Fig. 5-23. For a professional player, the high-speed stage is also the impact zone. A beginner who releases too early raises the upper edge of his high-speed stage to his waist level.

THE ANGLE OF THE NSP

The NSP inclines along the target line at an angle, which ideally should be the designed lie angle of the club used. In reality though, the actual angle of the NSP is not set in stone and can have a few degrees of variation from the ideal value.

A modern iron usually has rounded corners on its sole. Thus a deviation of a couple degrees in actual lie angle can be easily accommodated and will not affect ball striking noticeably.

Fig. 5-24   Rounded Bottom

A driver or a fairway wood has even greater tolerance because of its rounded bottom. Such a design allows a club to be placed on the ground with a wider range of acceptable lie positions.

In theory, deviating from the designed lie angle can affect the ball flight direction. That is why a golfer should aim right when the ball is above his feet because the lie angle is changed drastically. However, the influence on ball flight is limited when the lie deviation is insignificant.

For the reasons described above, the NSP angle for a given club can be the club's designed lie angle plus or minus a few degrees, as long as the setup is comfortable for the golfer.

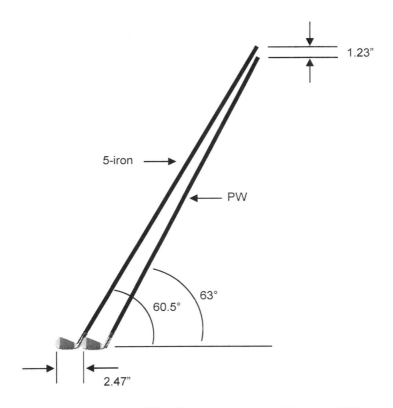

Fig. 5-25 NSP Difference between 5-iron and PW

Here is another interesting aspect: the NSPs for mid and short irons can be very similar. As an example, let's take a look at the Mizuno MP-59 irons. We will just look at the PW (pitching wedge) and the 5-iron, and skip the four in between (6, 7, 8, and 9 irons).

Mizuno MP-59 Irons

Club	5-iron	PW
Loft	27°	46°
Lie	60.5°	63°
Length	37.75"	35.50"

The lie angle difference between the 5-iron and the PW is only 2.5 degrees and the club length difference is 2.25 inches. When set up at their designed lie angles, the distance from the end of the club to the ground is 32.86 inches for the 5-iron and 31.63 inches for the PW. The difference between their ground clearances is only 1.23 inches.

It is obvious that there is no drastic change in posture or striking plane when switching from a PW to a 5-iron. Knowing this, a golfer should feel more comfortable when using a longer iron.

STEEP PLANE VS. FLAT PLANE

If two players set up similarly using the same club, their NSP angles should be quite close to each other with a couple degrees' difference in between at most. In other words, once a golfer sets up to a ball, his NSP angle is more or less determined. He cannot randomly switch to a striking plane that is much steeper or flatter afterwards by changing the motions of his arms in the backswing.

Then what on earth do people mean when they say a golfer can swing on steep or flat planes? With the same club, can one golfer really choose to swing on striking planes of significantly different angles?

The answer is no.

As we said earlier, the difference that people perceive from various swing styles is mainly determined by the range of plane deviation, i.e. how far the hands and club shift away from the NSP at the top of the backswing. A golfer who pushes the club much higher above the NSP appears to have a "steep" plane, whereas one who keeps his club closer to the NSP appears to swing on a "flat" one.

However, when it comes down to the most critical impact zone, good players of similar physical features (height and arm length, etc.) actually swing their clubs on very similar striking planes, if they set up similarly and use similar clubs.

A golfer might appear to swing on a striking plane that is much steeper than his SSP, but that is NOT really happening. Looking steep doesn't mean actually swinging on a steep plane.

In Fig. 5-26, both players have their SSPs at a 45-degree angle (SSPs are not shown here; please see swing examples in chapter seven). At the top, the hand-to-ball line is 57 degrees with reference to the ground for A and 52 degrees for B.

Without drastic posture change at impact, it is very difficult for player A to hit the ball solidly and consistently on a striking plane that is 12 degrees steeper than his SSP.

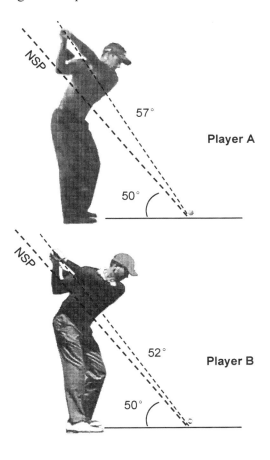

Fig. 5-26 Steep and Flat Swingers Have the Same NSP

As will be discussed in chapter seven, both players actually move their clubs on the same 50-degree NSP within the impact zone. Essentially, they have the SAME swing plane!

THE STRIKING PLANE FOR AN IRON

An iron, especially a mid or short iron, must strike slightly downward at impact to achieve solid contact. This can be evidenced by the target side divot typically seen in a solid iron shot.

As shown in Fig. 5-27, in a downward strike the clubhead hits the ball before it reaches the bottom of its swing arc. Its velocity at impact points both slightly downward and rightward. If a golfer aligns his striking plane perfectly with the target and strikes down perfectly with an iron, the ball will launch slightly toward the right of the target. To compensate this effect, he should aim slightly to the left of the flag. That is why the divot taken by a professional player in an iron shot usually points slightly to the left.

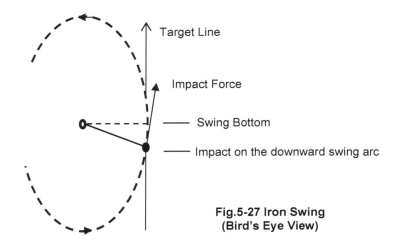

Fig.5-27 Iron Swing
(Bird's Eye View)

Let's look at the following scenario: a golfer has a 7-iron in his hands and the distance from his left shoulder to the clubhead is 55 inches. The clubhead bottoms out five inches in front of the ball, and the club has a lie angle of 60 degrees. According to geometric calculations, the clubhead at impact will be moving approximately 2.6 degrees to the right and 4.5 degrees down.

Theoretically, 2.6 degrees to the right translates into 7.3 yards off the target for a 160-yard shot if no side spin is involved.

THE STRIKING PLANE FOR A DRIVER

For a driver shot, the ball is on a tee and above the ground. The ball should be struck by the driver on the upward section of the swing arc. As shown in Fig. 5-28, the clubhead velocity at impact points slightly to the left if the ball is hit at the upswing arc,

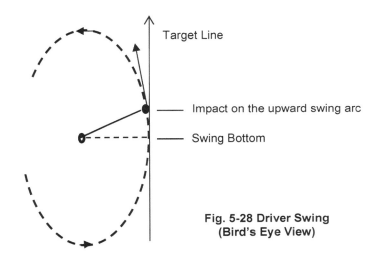

Target Line

Impact on the upward swing arc

Swing Bottom

**Fig. 5-28 Driver Swing
(Bird's Eye View)**

If a golfer aligns his striking plane precisely with the target and hits a perfect drive, the ball will launch at a small angle to the left of the flag.

Assuming a driver's clubhead is 65 inches away from the golfer's left shoulder at impact; the clubhead reaches the bottoms six inches behind the ball; and the club travels on a 50-degree striking plane, then at impact the clubhead moves approximately 3.4 degrees to the left and 4.0 degrees upward.

Theoretically, 3.4 degrees to the left translates into 17.8 yards left off the target for a 300-yard drive if no side spin is involved. To compensate this effect, the striking plane should point slightly to the right of the target for a driver shot.

In *Five Lessons*, Ben Hogan described a downswing plane that inclines at a shallower angle than the backswing plane and whose lateral axis points slightly to the right. What he felt actually matches the Striking Plane Swing Model perfectly. From the top, a golfer has to lower the club toward the NSP, so he feels as if the striking plane is lower. In addition, he points the plane to the right to compensate the upswing offset for the driver. Although in reality the striking plane (or downswing plane as Ben Hogan called it) didn't rest on his shoulders and the right shoulder drop in the downswing wasn't the reason why the plane should be pointing to the right of the target.

A SUMMARY OF THE STRIKING PLANE SWING MODEL

Based on the knowledge of classical mechanics and human anatomy, the *Striking Plane Swing Model* describes the proper sequence of club movement, as well as the key requirements for consistent and solid ball striking, in a *conventional* golf swing.

To recapture what have been discussed in this chapter, the key points of the model are summarized as follows:

1. The whole club must travel on plane within the impact zone to deliver stable, predictable, and consistent shots. This plane is called the Striking Plane (KP).

2. A club does not necessarily return to its Setup Shaft Plane (SSP) at impact. Within the impact zone it should ideally move along the Normal Striking Plane (NSP), which is typically steeper than the SSP.

3. A golfer cannot swing his club on one plane throughout a full backswing. The club will be moved above the NSP at the top due to anatomical limitations.

4. A golfer cannot swing his club on one plane throughout a full downswing. The club is above the NSP at the top and must be dropped onto it before entering the impact zone.

96

5. A swing plane by its traditional definition does not exist. There is only the striking plane.

6. The angle of a striking plane should be approximately the designed lie angle of the club used. For a given club, a golfer cannot significantly change the steepness of the striking plane.

7. To achieve maximum clubhead speed, the club should be released in a compact striking slot.

8. During the downswing, the club moves at a lower speed above the impact zone while it is in the process of finding the proper alignment. It moves at a higher speed after entering the impact zone where it accelerates and releases.

9. The style of a swing is mainly determined by the backswing route and the range of plane deviation. The essence of a swing is determined by what happens within the impact zone.

6. SWING ANALYSIS

Video is a great way to evaluate golf swings and is an effective tool for game improvement. However, a golfer must use the proper method to analyze his swing video in order to retrieve the right information. If the method of analysis is flawed then the feedback can be misleading or even detrimental.

In this chapter, we will discuss the *SPM Swing Analysis,* i.e. swing analysis using the Striking Plane Swing Model.

THE PRESENT SWING ANALYSIS METHODS

There appears to be no standard for swing analysis in the golf community at the time of writing. Every instructor may have his own opinions and approaches for analysis and the conclusions often vary or even contradicting. Many of the existing swing analysis methods often have difficulty explaining the unorthodox but working swing styles among professional players.

A commonly seen swing analysis method involves drawing a line between the ball and the golfer's shoulder joint, as shown in Fig. 6-1. This line is then used as the main reference for the whole swing. Few people have ever questioned the validity of this method.

Some instructors introduced an even more complex method that involves three lines, which represent the so-called hand plane (or shaft plane), elbow plane (or right arm plane), and shoulder plane respectively. They believe golfers can swing down on their shoulder plane, which can be 15 degrees away from their SSP. Since a shoulder plane or elbow plane cannot be defined precisely, we have to wonder how accurate the analyses can be.

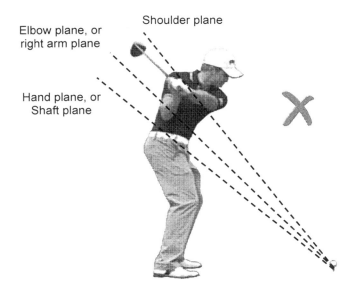

Fig. 6-1 Existing Swing Analysis Methods

Swing Analysis Using the Striking Plane Model

Golf is a game that values precision and golf swings should be analyzed precisely. Swing analysis using the Striking Plane Swing Model is simple and accurate. It needs only one essential reference line and one optional reference line and we know exactly where these lines should be drawn. The analysis can show exactly what the problems are.

To get accurate and meaningful results from a swing analysis, it is critical that the swing video be recorded properly and the right software program be used. We will go over a few key areas below.

Choosing the Right Camera

A clubhead moves at a very high speed (80~120 mph) in a golf swing. A regular digital camera, which typically records videos at only 30 frames per second (fps), is not capable of capturing enough information for analysis. The regular speed recording may also introduce sampling distortion, in which a straight shaft could look severely bent. Such video clips are only suitable for general purpose swing evaluations.

For accurate swing analyses, videos should ideally be recorded at a frame rate of 240 fps or higher. Some consumer digital cameras can record low resolution videos at 240 fps and are acceptable for recreational use. I have also used a high-end smartphone camera, which can record at 120 fps with a much higher resolution, for some of the pictures in this book.

It is highly recommended that a tripod be used to hold the camera during recording. This guarantees that a line drawn for reference stay at the same location in every frame of the video. If a person has to hold the camera by hand for the recording, he should make every effort to keep the camera steady during the critical two seconds. Keeping the arms close to the body and holding the breath may be helpful.

The Views

A swing video can be recorded from many different angles, but only two camera views are commonly used for golf swing analyses, they are:

- Face-on view (FO)
- Down-the-line view (DTL)

For face-on view, the camera is placed in front of the golfer. Videos from this view are mainly used to evaluate the lag, release, angle of attack, and swing bottom of the club etc. They can also be used to check the golfer's posture and the movement of his head, arms, wrists, legs, and hips.

For down-the-line view, the camera is placed on the right side of the (right-handed) golfer and points down the target line. Videos recorded from down-the-line view are typically used to check the swing plane.

Since swing plane is the focus of this book, we mainly use videos and pictures taken from down-the-line view.

Camera Setup

The position and angle of the camera are not so important for face-on videos, but very critical for down-the-line recording and should be given careful considerations.

From down-the-line view, improper camera positions or angles can make swing analysis inaccurate or even impossible. For example, if the camera is placed too far to the right, a club traveling on plane may appear to be moving from inside to outside. It is important that the camera be placed at the proper location, set to the right height, and pointed to the correct direction to get the best results.

Here is an effective way to find the right camera position and angle: place a 4'x2' wood panel at a 60-degree angle against the ground and use it as a visual representation of the NSP, then adjust the camera location, height, and angle until the wood panel shows up as a line in the camera viewfinder. This would be the proper position for the camera and you should remember how it is related to your stance.

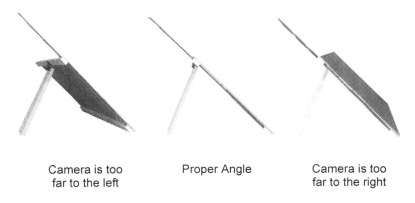

| Camera is too far to the left | Proper Angle | Camera is too far to the right |

Fig. 6-2 Camera Angle Test

I usually put the camera at waist level and place it on the extension of my foot line (parallel to the target line). The camera should point straight to the intended target.

The telescopic end of a zoom lens has less optical distortion than the wide-angle end and is the preferred setting in swing video recording. I usually put the camera as far away from the golfer as reasonably possible, and then zoom in to get the proper frame.

Since ball flight and shot quality may not always be visible in the video, golfers should design a set of gestures to signal the shot information so you can establish the correlation between a particular swing video and the actual ball flight for analyses. The gestures should at least cover straight, hook, slice, fat, and thin shots.

Swing Analysis Software

A special software program is required to review and analyze the golf swing videos. Such a program should have at least the following functions:

- Manual frame by frame video playback
- Line drawing
- Angle measurement

Some other functions are also desirable because they make it possible to perform more advanced tasks. However, they are not critical to basic analyses.

- Side by side comparison
- Object tracing
- Video trimming
- Timer
- Playback speed adjustment
- Image capture

Most of the commercial software programs designed for golf swing analysis can meet all these requirements. Some free open-source programs are also available for golf swing analysis.

STEP ONE: DEFINING THE SSP

Once the video is loaded into the software, we will fast forward it to the point immediately before the takeaway and then draw a straight line along the club shaft. The line should extend through the golfer's body, as show in Fig. 6-3. Either a solid line or a dash line can be used.

This line represents the SSP (Setup Shaft Plane) from the DTL (Down-the-Line) view and will be used as an optional reference line.

Although the SSP line is not absolutely required in swing analyses using the Striking Plane Swing Model, it can be useful as a reference in analyzing certain swing faults, such as the notorious shank.

Fig. 6-3 Defining the SSP

STEP TWO: DEFINING THE NSP

In this step, we are going to define the NSP (Normal Striking Plane) line of the swing. First fast forward the video to the moment of impact. You might have noticed that the shaft is not straight as it approaches the ball. This is not caused by the gravity as many people have claimed. If you hold a club still in the air, the gravity barely causes any shaft drooping.

This phenomenon is the result of the high speed swing. For a typical club, the COG (center of gravity) of the clubhead is not in line with its shaft and will be pulled toward the shaft plane during a high speed swing. This causes the shaft tip to bend downward.

Fig. 6-4 Defining the NSP

The proper NSP therefore should overlap the upper section of the club shaft and cross the COG of the clubhead. Since the COG is near the center of the clubhead and is behind the sweet spot, we will draw a straight line from the sweet spot to the club grip, and extend it through the golfer's body, as shown in Fig. 6-4. In a perfect shot, the sweet spot of the clubface should be right against the ball so this line may seems to go across the ball.

This line represents the NSP and is an essential reference line in swing analyses.

104

STEP THREE: REVIEWING THE PLANE RELATION

With the SSP and NSP lines in place, the first thing we should do is checking their angular relation. We will use the tool in the swing analysis software to measure the angle between the two lines. The reading should typically be less than seven degrees. If you see an angle of 10 degrees between them then the NSP is probably too steeper than the SSP. This means the hands at impact might have moved too high above their positions at setup. The golfer would have to make extra change to his posture at impact in order to hit solid. This could be a probable cause for inconsistency and off-center shots, especially heel shots and shanks

STEP FOUR: REVIEWING THE TAKEAWAY

Now we are going rewind the video back to the beginning of the swing and review the takeaway. In an ideal takeaway, the club should move up along the space between the SSP and NSP, as shown in Fig. 6-5.

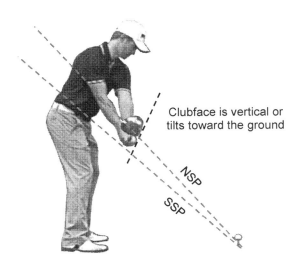

Clubface is vertical or tilts toward the ground

Fig. 6-5 Club Position at the End of Takeaway

The golfer should mainly rely on his upper body turn to move the club away in order to achieve a more powerful coil. If this is done properly, the clubhead will naturally move along the target line for the first 12~24 inches. This is taught by many instructors as the "one-piece takeaway."

From the DTL view, we should see the club shaft move along or slightly above the SSP line all the way to the point where it is parallel to the ground. This position marks the completion of the takeaway. Here the club can be on the SSP and points straight to the right, or it can be a little above the SSP and point slightly away from the plane. Both cases are commonly seen among professional players.

However, the club should not drop below the SSP significantly as we have discussed before. Such a detour is totally unnecessary and can easily cause many issues. On the other hand, getting the hands and club well above the NSP is also a sign of trouble and is more concerning than an inside takeaway.

At the completion of the takeaway, the clubface should either be vertical or face the ground. It should not face the sky.

STEP FIVE: REVIEWING THE UPPER BACKSWING

Once passing the parallel position, the club will start moving above the SSP to avoid the restrictions from the right elbow and right wrist. During this stage, please check if the shaft maintains a positive angle (steeper) with reference to the SSP. The shaft should not be flatter than the SSP during the backswing.

At the top of a full swing, the club should ideally be parallel to the ground, as well as to the target line, and point to the target. It is therefore parallel to the SSP or NSP. This position makes it easier for the club to drop onto the NSP during the downswing.

If the club is pointing away from the target on the top, the golfer can still make adjustment during the downswing to hit a straight shot, but he is prone to make mistakes.

Here we should also evaluate the range of plane deviation. Many beginners tend to have a shorter range. The modern tour pros often have a longer range. I personally strike the ball better with my left arm raised high above my right shoulder.

106

STEP SIX: REVIEWING THE KEY MOVE IN DOWNSWING

During the initial downswing, the golfer should be seen quickly bringing the club down towards the NSP in an effort to align it with the striking slot. Check the video to see if the golfer gets the club onto the NSP before the quarter-swing position.

A club that is still above the NSP at the quarter-swing position will very likely have trouble entering the striking slot consistently. The golfer will often hit the ball from an outside-in direction, which will either produce a slice/fade or a pull, depending on the clubface orientation.

A beginner or a slicer should pay special attention to this step. If the club gets on the NSP as expected and there is still slice, then the problem comes from an open clubface at impact. Many beginners have both outside-in downswing and open clubface at impact. This evil combination will guarantee to produce a severe slice with a low-loft club, such as a driver or a fairway wood.

A player whose club drops below the NSP at the quarter-swing position will probably fail to enter the striking slot also, and will hit the ball from an inside-out direction, which will either produce a hook/draw or a push.

STEP SEVEN: REVIEWING THE RELEASE AND IMPACT

Starting from the quarter-swing position in the downswing, the club should stay on the NSP perfectly in order to hit a straight and pure shot. The line representing the NSP should be seen overlapping the club shaft all the way through impact and a little beyond. The ability to swing and release a club on plane within the impact zone differentiates a good player from a poor one.

This is where the Striking Plane Swing Model analysis outperforms other swing analysis methods. With a roughly drawn shoulder line or elbow line as the reference, it is impossible to tell whether or not the club is off track by a small amount because these lines are irrelevant to the club movement within the impact zone and they cannot be precisely defined either.

STEP EIGHT: REVIEWING POST-IMPACT CLUB POSITION

After impact, the club shaft should still be seen moving on the NSP until both arms have fully extended. This is the indication of a good on-plane swing.

If the club has been released properly, the arms should cross over soon after impact. The arm crossover can be better seen in a face-on video. Once the arms cross over after impact, the club will start rising above the NSP in the follow-through due to the left elbow restriction.

7. SWING ANALYSIS EXAMPLES

Now that we are familiar with the swing analysis procedures using the Striking Plane Swing Model, it is time to take a test drive with some real world examples. In this chapter, we are going to analyze some typical golf swings using this simple and accurate method.

To further prove the validity of the model, the swing examples we are going to analyze include many different styles: older school, modern, orthodox, unconventional, "steep," "flat," professional, and amateur.

People often talk about the fundamentals of the golf swing. What exactly is a fundamental? Apparently, a true fundamental of golf swing must be something all great ball strikers have in common. After reading this chapter, I am sure you will be able to draw your own conclusions.

Some of the images used here were posed or emulated by our golfer models. Some were reconstructed or synthesized based on low-resolution swing videos and may still appear blurry after software enhancement. Even though these pictures serve the purpose well, we do wish they could have been in higher resolutions.

There are many unique swing styles that are worth analyzing. However, we will only able to present a few typical ones here due to our limited resources. Readers who have a broader collection of swing videos are encouraged to conduct more analyses using the techniques discussed in this book. I am confident that you will find the Striking Plane Swing Model true and valuable and the associated method of analysis simple and effective.

Ben Hogan's Swing Analysis

Ben Hogan is one of the greatest players in the history of golf and is a legendary ball striker. He is also considered to have a profound influence on the golf swing theory.

Here we are going to analyze Mr. Hogan's swing using the Striking Plane Swing Model. Some of the things you read here might not be in total agreement with what Mr. Hogan had written in his book. Nonetheless, please keep in mind that *Five Lessons* is still a great golf book, especially if you learn to follow its spirit, rather than just the letter.

Due to the lack of high-speed cameras in Hogan's time, true slow motion videos of Ben Hogan are not available. The pictures below were reconstructed using computer programs to represent Ben Hogan's actual swing.

Setup

This is Ben Hogan's iron setup. The dash line represents his SSP, which is also his NSP. Please notice that Ben Hogan's arms extend slightly to the ball. In this particular swing, his upper body was not bent as much as in his driver setup, in which the angle between the upper body and the club was nearly 90 degrees.

NSP = SSP

Fig. 7-1 Iron Setup

51°

Takeaway

Ben Hogan's club is often slightly below the SSP during the takeaway, but nothing serious in this swing.

Fig. 7-2 Takeaway

Backswing

Ben Hogan's hands and club are above the SSP half way in the backswing.

Fig. 7-3 Backswing

111

Top of Backswing

Ben Hogan's left arm and the club are well above the SSP at the top of the backswing. Only at this point is his left arm close to the "backswing plane" (shoulder plane) he described in *Five Lessons*.

**Fig. 7-4
Top of Backswing**

Downswing

Ben Hogan usually gets his club onto the NSP very early in downswing but not in this one. His club is laid off a little at the start of the downswing and still is at this point in this swing.

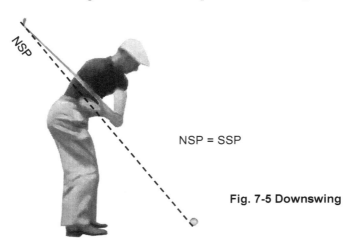

NSP = SSP

Fig. 7-5 Downswing

Impact

At impact, Ben Hogan's club returns to the NSP, which is the same as his SSP.

50°

Fig. 7-6 Impact

Summary

There are several interesting points about Ben Hogan's swing. First, his NSP is the same as his SSP. That means he returns his club back to the setup plane at impact. This is actually quite uncommon among golfers and there are only a handful of professional players who exhibit this feature.

Backswing Plane: In *Five Lessons*, Ben Hogan described a "backswing plane" that runs from the ball to his shoulders (the solid lines in Fig. 7-7) and stated that the left arm should be parallel to this plane above the hip level and brush it at the top of the backswing. However, if we trace Ben Hogan's arm movement during the backswing, we will notice that his left arm neither brushes against nor stays parallel to this plane at the top of his backswing, as evidenced by the pictures in Fig. 7-7.

Apparently, the famous pane of glass resting on Ben Hogan's shoulders is not his actual backswing plane. In fact, although his club moves rather close to the SSP in the lower half of the backswing, there is no plane for his entire backswing.

Fig. 7-7 The Backswing Plane

We can also notice that Ben Hogan's left shoulder pokes out of the "backswing plane" at the top but his right shoulder is far beneath it. This contradicts his statement "the top of the shoulders will continuously be brushing against the glass."

At the top of his backswing, Ben Hogan's left arm is usually quite low and gives people the impression of "being flat," although in this swing his range is greater by his own standard. Like many other great players, his shoulder line is not perpendicular to his spine.

Downswing Plane: Ben Hogan described a "downswing plane," which also rests on his shoulders but inclines at a slightly narrower angle than the "backswing plane" due to the posture change at downswing. Again, if we trace his movement, his club or left arm never travels on this shoulder plane during the downswing. *It is evident that this more inclined downswing shoulder plane is not his actual downswing plane.* In fact, most of the time during downswing his club travels on his SSP, which is much lower than the shoulder plane. Mr. Hogan might have felt the "downswing plane" being flatter because of the club dropping action in the early downswing. However, in the video he does just the opposite: his club path in downswing is actually slightly steeper than that in the backswing.

114

Usually, Ben Hogan's club returned to the NSP starting from the half-swing position and is earlier than most players; however, he is a little bit late in this swing. Most modern day professional golfers return their clubs back to their NSPs around the quarter-swing position. As we said before, being able to return the club back on plane sooner is advantageous. A golfer who does this can be more consistent in ball striking, especially when he is under pressure.

STEEP VS. FLAT

What do people actually mean when they talk about steep swing and flat swing? Let's find out. Here we are going to compare the swings of two professional players who are believed to have distinctively different swing styles.

Player A is considered by many as a golfer with a "steep" swing plane, whereas player B is deemed to have a "flat" swing. Player A is commonly considered as a "two-plane" golfer and B as a "one-plane" player according to Jim Hardy's definitions.

With the existing swing analysis methods, which do not typically touch the essence of the swing plane, such classifications seem to make sense and match what we saw. At the top of the backswing, if we draw lines from their hands to the ball then player A's line is definitely steeper. But, do these lines really represent what actually happens in their swings, especially within the impact zone?

Let's find out by analyzing their swings using the Striking Plane Swing Model. To compare apple to apple, we are going to look at their driver swings.

Player A is an exemplar of the modern mainstream tour players who conduct a textbook conventional swing, such as Tiger Woods, Adam Scott, and Jason Day etc.

Player B represents the players who have a less popular "flat" swing, such as Matt Kuchar and Ben Hogan.

In this particular case, player B is three inches taller than player A. It is reasonable to assume that player B has a greater tendency to execute a "steeper" swing. Apparently, that was not the case.

Setup

At setup, both players have similar postures. Their upper bodies are nearly perpendicular to the SSP. Player B does bend forward a little more as he is taller. Their hands hang down freely. Both of their SSPs incline at 45 degrees and run through their waists. Both of their NSPs are steeper and incline at an angle of 50 degrees.

Fig. 7-8 Setup

Backswing

During the backswing, a significant difference develops. At the top, player A's left arm is much steeper than his shoulder line and appears to have a very steep swing plane, whereas B's left arm matches his shoulder line and appears to be flat. A's range of plane deviation is much greater than B's. As a result, A's hands are closer to the front, while B's hands are well behind.

The line from A's hands to the ball is 56 degrees to the ground; whereas B's line is 51 degrees. This is the main reason their swings appear to be very different.

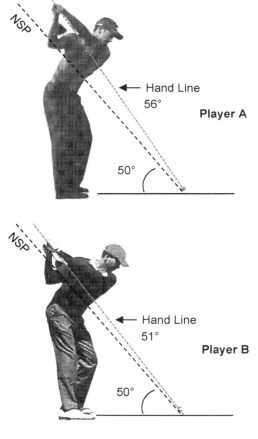

Fig. 7-9 Top of Backswing

Downswing

As soon as the downswing starts, both players drop their clubs toward their NSPs (both incline at 50 degrees). Surprisingly, player A, who has a greater range to shift, gets his club onto the NSP perfectly at the half-swing position, whereas player B still has his club above the NSP at the same position.

From this point on, both players have very similar postures and moves. Nobody would say one has a steeper swing than the other.

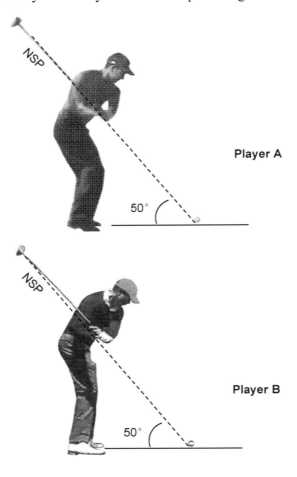

Fig. 7-10 Downswing

Entering the Slot

When the clubs are parallel to the ground and about to enter the striking slots, both players have nearly identical postures and club positions. Their hands are on the NSP, although B's clubhead is slightly above the plane. Both players keep their upper bodies 90 degrees to the NSPs.

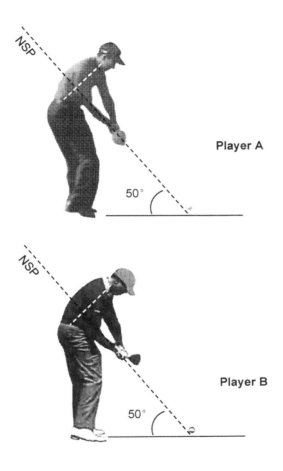

Fig. 7-11 Parallel Position

Impact

At impact, both players have similar postures and the clubs travel on NSPs of the same angle. By looking at these pictures, we honestly cannot say player A has a steeper swing plane than player B. In fact, they aren't much different within the impact zone.

After impact, both players continue moving their clubs along their NPSs until their arms are both in full extension.

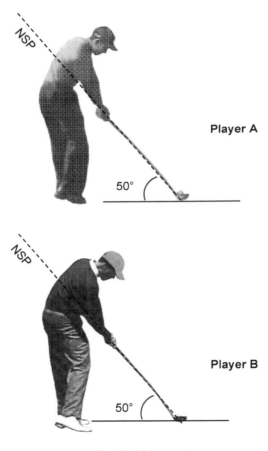

Fig. 7-12 Impact

Summary

Even though these two players appear to have drastically different swings, their NSPs have identical angle of inclination, so do their SSPs.

 Within the impact zone, where the quality of a shot is ultimately determined, there is no significant difference between their postures, club positions, or swing movements!

 The main difference lies in the range of plane deviation at the top of the backswing, but that is about it. The range affects power, timing, and style. However, it doesn't necessarily have any correlation with the angle of the striking plane.

 The conclusions we arrive at is shocking: both players have the same setup posture, the same SSP, the same NSP, and their moves within the critical impact zone are nearly identical. *As far as the swing plane is concerned, both players are the same. Neither is steeper than the other.*

 This example of swing analysis tells us that our impression can be misleading sometimes. We cannot always judge things based on what we see or feel.

Loop Swing Analysis

Player C has a very unique but working swing style. Many people have been wondering why someone can violate so many "rules" or "fundamentals" of a textbook swing and still hit great shots. Actually, according to the Striking Plane Swing Model, Player C's swing might appear unconventional, but is technically flawless. Within the impact zone, his move meets every fundamental requirement and is no different from other pros.

This again shows that our eyes are unable to capture the high speed details of a swing and our impression is often based upon what we see at the low speed stage.

Setup

Player C has a conventional setup with some unique features. The dash line represents his SSP, which goes *under* his belt. His hands are very close to his thighs, a feature Sergio Garcia also exhibits. With a driver in his hands, the inclination angle of his SSP is about 46 degrees.

Fig. 7-13 Setup

Takeaway

His takeaway is slightly below the SSP. But once the club passes the parallel-to-ground position, he moves it up almost vertically.

Fig. 7-14 Takeaway

Backswing

Here is his signature move half way in the backswing: the club points straight to the sky with its butt pointing at his foot line.

Fig. 7-15 Swinging Up

123

Top of Backswing

His left arm points to the sky at the top of the backswing. The darker dash line represents his NSP, which is 53° to the ground.

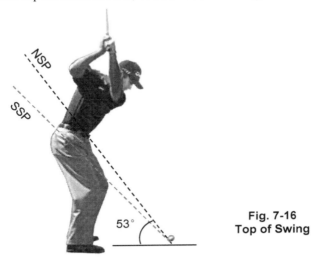

Fig. 7-16
Top of Swing

Downswing

He lowers his club onto the striking plane via a loop action. His club has turned parallel to the NSP at the half-swing position.

Fig. 7-17
Club Coming Down

Entering the Slot

At the entrance to the striking slot, he finally gets the club on the NSP.

Fig. 7-18
Entering the Slot

Impact

At impact, his body is more open than others; he is almost facing the target.

Fig. 7-19 Impact

125

Post Impact

After impact, his club still moves along the NSP. This confirms that his swing within the impact zone is perfectly on plane.

Fig. 7-20 Post Impact

Summary

Although player C's swing appears to be unorthodox, his movements inside the critical impact zone is flawless and no different than other great players'. That is why he can hit great shots and win. He further proves that the backswing path of the club is not a fundamental element in ball striking, swinging the club on a striking plane within the impact zone is.

The angle between his SSP and NSP is seven (7) degrees, which is on the high side among professional players. This is probably the result of his very open upper body position at impact.

His club gets on the NSP near the entrance to the striking slot. This is relatively late compare to other tour pros.

An average golfer will be better off learning a textbook conventional swing, because the way player C moves his club onto the NSP requires extraordinary coordination, and can be error-prone for average golfers.

126

DRAW SWING ANALYSIS

Shot shaping is an advanced skill for golfers. In the swing example below, Dan Courtney, co-author of the book, demonstrates how to hit a draw, in which the ball curves from right to left due to a counter clockwise side spin. To produce such a side spin, a golfer can swing his club from inside to outside and keep the clubface square to the target line at impact; or he can swing on plane but keep the clubface closed at impact.

Setup

The lighter dash line represents Dan' SSP; the darker one is his NSP. The angle between the two planes is approximately 7 degrees. The angle between his upper body and the club shaft is very close to 90 degrees.

In this example, Dan will swing the club from inside (under the NSP) to outside at impact.

Fig. 7-21 Setup

127

Takeaway

During the takeaway, Dan moves his club below his SSP, preparing for an inside-out downswing.

Fig. 7-22 Takeaway

Backswing

Half way through the backswing, his club moves above the SSP to overcome the blockage, but is still below the NSP.

Fig. 7-23 Backswing

Top of Backswing

At the top of his backswing, Dan's club moves above the NSP as well to get more power. His left arm is much steeper than his shoulder line and his range of deviation is significant.

Fig. 7-24
Backswing Top

Downswing

At the quarter-swing position, Dan's hands are on the NSP, but his club is still below and moving along an inside-out path.

Fig. 7-25
Quarter Swing Position

129

Entering the Impact Zone

Before entering the impact zone, his hands are on plane, but his club is still below the NSP, which his actual striking plane will cut across.

Fig. 7-26
Entering Impact Zone

Before Impact

Right before impact, Dan's club is still below the NSP and will strike the ball from an inside-out direction. His actual striking plane cuts across the NSP and points slightly to the right of the target.

Fig. 7-27
Before Impact

Impact

At impact, His actual striking plane intersects the NSP, on which the club stays momentarily. To guarantee a draw, the clubface must be closed to the swing direction at impact.

Fig. 7-28 Impact

Post Impact

After impact, the club moves above the NSP. This further confirms the inside-out impact direction. The ball launches to the right and then curves back to the left.

**Fig. 7-29
Post Impact**

SLICE SWING ANALYSIS

Slice is a notorious problem among golfers, especially beginners. We have thoroughly discussed the reason behind it in the previous chapters. Golfers can understand and fix this headache by learning the correct swing plane model and the proper sequence of club movement.

In the following example, amateur golfer Curtis Metcalf demonstrates hitting a slice shot with the driver. This time we are going to conduct the swing analysis using only the NSP line.

Setup

The dash line represents Curtis' NSP, which is just above his club shaft at setup. You will notice that Curtis has a very upright posture. The angle between his upper body and the club is much greater than 90 degrees.

With his upright posture, Curtis' NSP passes through his upper body above his elbow rest point and inclines at 46 degrees.

Fig. 7-30 Setup

Takeaway

During the takeaway, Curtis' club stays very close to his NSP. His arms are already bent at this stage.

Fig. 7-31 Takeaway

Backswing

Half way through the backswing, he is still able to keep his club on the NSP thanks to his upright posture

Fig. 7-32 Backswing

Top of Backswing

At the top, Curtis' club also moves above the NSP to overcome the blockage. His left arm is much steeper than his shoulder line but his range of deviation is limited due to his upright posture.

Fig. 7-33 Top of Backswing

Downswing

Half way through his downswing, his club is still high above the NSP and over his right shoulder, a typical over-the-top move.

Fig. 7-34 Half Way in Downswing

Entering the Impact Zone

A moment before entering the impact zone, his hands and club are still above the NSP. There is not enough time left for correction.

Fig. 7-35 Entering the Impact Zone

Before Impact

Right before impact, Curtis' hands are on the NSP but his clubhead is still outside the plane. This is a typical outside-in downswing. A slice or a pull is unavoidable depending on his clubface orientation.

Fig. 7-36 Before Impact

135

Impact

At impact, his actual striking plane cuts across the NSP, on which the club stays momentarily. A big slice is about to be produced.

Fig. 7-37 Impact

Post Impact

After impact, the club moves below the NSP and the ball launches slightly to the left. This further confirms the outside-in impact direction. This swing indeed produced a huge slice.

Fig. 7-38 Post Impact

Summary

This is a typical outside-in or over-the-top downswing commonly seen among golfers who have not learned the proper downswing movement. Curtis attacks the ball via a straight line from the top and his actual striking plane points to the left of the target and cuts across the NSP, on which his club is supposed to travel to hit a straight shot. What is missing in Curtis' swing is the critical first move in the downswing: lowering the club toward the NSP.

MOE NORMAN'S SWING ANALYSIS

Moe Norman, a Canadian golfer, is well-known for his one of a kind swing style and extraordinary ball striking skills. His swing would have been a great subject for analysis. However, due to the lack of his slow motion videos from the proper angle, only a summary is provided here. Readers who have access to better quality video clips for Mr. Norman can analyze his swing as a home assignment.

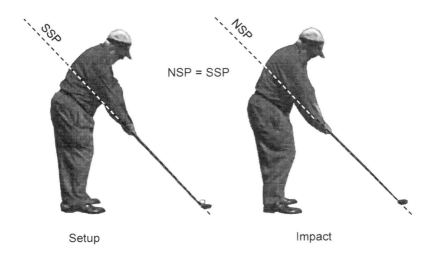

Setup   Impact

Fig. 7-39 Moe Norman's Swing

137

Summary

Moe Norman has an *unconventional* setup, in which his arms extend toward the ball and forms a straight line with the club. The dash line on the left of Fig. 7-39 represents his SSP, which passes through his body *above* his elbow rest point.

Moe Norman's setup is unique in the way that he raises his SSP above his elbow rest point. By doing this, he can avoid the blockage from the right elbow and right wrist. Moe Norman's NSP is nearly identical to his SSP and his swing is very close to a robot-style one-plane swing.

He usually finishes his backswing somewhere between the half-swing and three-quarter swing positions. Sometimes, his club is on the SSP at the top, but has also been seen above it in some cases.

He does not rotate his body aggressively during the downswing. At impact, Moe's club returns to the SSP. His body is not as open to the target as many other professional players' are.

I personally think this is because he set up with the club and his arms fully extended on a straight line so there was no slack from his should to the ball. He would miss the ball if his body were open at impact with his left shoulder moving away from its setup position. This perhaps is the reason why Moe was not a long hitter, although he hit very straight shots.

Nonetheless, Moe Norman's club stays on the SSP throughout the impact zone and his swing exhibits all the essential elements defined by the Striking Plane Swing Model.

8. SWING PLANE TRAINING TOOLS

SWING PLANE GUIDE

A swing plane guide is a type of training aid used to direct the club movement so a golfer can get familiar with the correct club positions in a golf swing.

Although many types of swing plane guide are commercially available, only a few are based on the fundamentally correct swing plane model. The rest would not work as expected or might even teach a user the wrong swing movement.

How do we determine whether or not a swing plane guide is properly designed? According to the Striking Plane Swing Model, a good swing plane guide should have a planar component in its lower section. Otherwise, it will fail to teach a user to swing the whole club on a plane within the impact zone.

If the golfer is only required to move the clubhead along a single-rail guide, then there is no guarantee that his entire club travels on plane within the impact zone. If his hands are below the plane, a golfer could actually build a tendency to hit a slice or fade.

For a golfer who uses a conventional setup, the club does not travel on one plane the entire time, so a swing plane guide that requires him to keep the clubhead on a single circular rail (as shown in Fig. 8-1) throughout a full swing is either set up on an inappropriate angle or teaching the wrong move at the top, unless the intention is to teach the Moe Norman swing style.

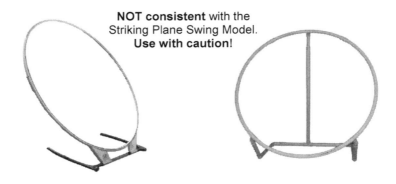

NOT consistent with the
Striking Plane Swing Model.
Use with caution!

Fig 8-1   Single-rail Swing Plane Guides

A swing plane guide with a planar lower section, such as the one shown in Fig. 8-2, will do a better job teaching the correct swing plane concept. Bear in mind though, these types of train aid may still have a drawback, because the striking plane is usually steeper than the setup shaft plane for most golfers. Nonetheless, they will teach the users the proper takeaway path and the correct swing feel. You can easily build one like this at home using materials from home improvement stores.

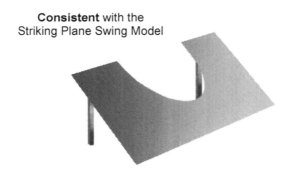

Consistent with the
Striking Plane Swing Model

Fig 8-2   A Swing Plane Guide with a Planar Lower Section

For a golfer with a conventional setup, he must also understand that the club should rise above the plane guide once it passes the parallel-to-ground position. This is the proper way of using a swing plane guide.

MIRROR

A mirror provides instant visual feedback on your swing, including your posture and the club position, so you can make corrections right away. It is an inexpensive yet valuable training aid. A golfer should check his swing through a mirror every so often.

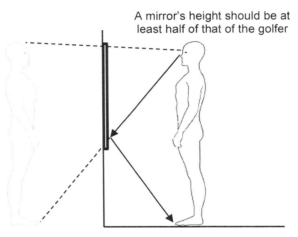

A mirror's height should be at least half of that of the golfer

Fig 8-3   Mirror

The theory of optics tells us that a mirror should be at least half of the viewer's height for him to see his whole body. For swing training purposes, a suitable mirror should be at least two feet in width and half of your height plus one foot in height so you can see the club as well. Needless to say, a wall mirror is the best option if that is available to you.

LASER POINTER

According to the Striking Plane Swing Model, the entire club should be moving along a plane below the quart-swing position to deliver a predictable strike. Some players naturally have good spatial perception and can accurately sense their club orientation during the swing, yet many others don't. The good news is that the spatial perception can be improved through training.

141

To improve our ability to sense the club orientation, we must be able to verify where the club is pointing. A laser pointer is the perfect tool for checking club alignment and it provides us with instant visual feedback.

Laser pointers specifically designed for golf swing training are available and can be mounted on the end of any golf club. Fig. 8-4 shows a typical laser pointer for golf.

Fig. 8-4   A Swing Laser Pointer

A swing laser pointer is essentially the same as those used in business presentations. They are just low-wattage laser transmitters powered by cell batteries.

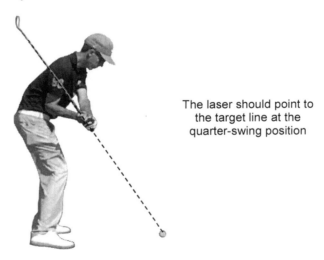

The laser should point to the target line at the quarter-swing position

Fig. 8-5 Checking Plane Alignment with a Laser Pointer

If a club stays on the NSP, the laser dot should move along the target line starting from the quarter-swing position until the club is parallel to the ground, providing a laser pointer is installed on the

142

end of the club and aligned properly. However, the other way around is not necessarily true: having the laser pointing to the target line does not guarantee the club is moving on a plane. For example, at the quarter-swing position, you can move your hands away from the NSP and still have the laser pointing down to the target line by adjusting the club orientation. The main use of a laser pointer is to help you verify the club alignment at certain point so you can fine tune your spatial perception.

If you are a handy person and love building things, you can get a good quality keychain laser pointer for about ten dollars and install it on a practice club. A good quality laser pointer should have the light pointing along its body center axis. Many inexpensive toy laser pointers will not meet this important requirement.

The pictures in Fig. 8-6 show you how a keychain laser pointer is installed on a practice club. First cut off the end of the grip to expose the metal shaft. This particular laser pointer, when wrapped with a couple layers of electrical tape, can fit perfectly inside a steel shaft. Since the pointer sits inside the shaft with a tight fit, the laser should point perfectly along the axis of the club shaft.

A mini laser pointer installed in the shaft

Fig. 8-6 A mini laser pointer

A cable tie or other mechanism can be used to hold down the push button to turn on the laser. The cable tie loop has a corner near the joint, which can be used to turn off the laser if it is right over the push button.

A laser pointer will fail to serve its purpose if the laser points away from the axis of the shaft. Always check the laser alignment along a straight line, such as a wall or the baseboard in a house, to make sure the laser points along the axis of the club shaft.

VIDEO CAMERA

A video camera is a precious tool in golf swing training. Since a club moves at a very high speed within the impact zone, choosing the right camera is critical. A typical consumer digital camera records video clips at only 30 frames per second (fps) and is far from sufficient for capturing the details of club movement.

Cameras that are capable of 240 fps video recording are sufficient for recreational use. Several consumer digital cameras are capable of recording video clips at 240 fps or higher and are available at very reasonable prices.

Both Casio and Canon manufacture consumer digital cameras that can record slow motion videos at 240 fps or greater. Some models even come with line drawing functions for on-camera swing analysis.

Certain smartphones, such as iPhone 5S, support 120 fps (slo-mo) video recording and can also be used for swing training purpose.

Fig. 8-7 Cameras with Slow Motion Recording

9. SWING PLANE DRILLS

Learning the correct swing plane model is only the first step in the journey to a better game. In order to develop the ability to swing a club on plane within the impact zone and the skills to hit great shots consistently, a golfer must also practice diligently.

There are many drills for swing plane training. A few effective ones are listed here to help golfers practice and ingrain the proper sequence of movement, or improve their ability to swing a club on plane.

THE BASEBALL SWING DRILL

The baseball swing drill is also known as the horizontal swing plane drill. It can help golfers develop and improve the ability to visualize a swing plane. For many people, it is much easier to envision a plane that is leveled.

A beginner often fails to cross over his forearms as he releases the club. In this drill, a golfer must roll his right arm over the left in order to keep the club on plane after release. Otherwise, he would either push the club off the plane or have to bend his left arm to a "chicken wing" shape after impact.

To start this drill, take a normal upright stance and hold a club with the proper grip. Extend both arms in front of you and keep the club parallel to the ground at shoulder level, as shown in Fig. 9-1. You should always look at the front in this drill.

Now rotate your upper body clockwise to drive your arms and the club to the right side. Start cocking the wrists just like in a normal golf swing once the club passes your (original) right side.

145

Fig. 9-1 The Horizontal Swing Drill

Turn right as far as you can, meanwhile keep your left arm and the club on the same shoulder level horizontal plane. Your right elbow naturally points down.

Pause at the end of the clockwise rotation, and then rotate your body counterclockwise to take your left arm and the club along the same horizontal plane to your left. Once your hands pass your right foot, start uncocking the wrists and roll over your right forearm over the left one to release the club, which should stay on plane all the time. Keep turning your upper body counterclockwise to the finish position with both arms folded.

This drill can be a perfect warm-up routine for a practice session. It will certainly help beginners get rid of the post-impact "chicken wing."

Readers can also watch the Baseball Swing Drill, which was posted on YouTube by golf instructor David Leadbetter, to learn similar moves.

THE UPRIGHT GOLF SWING DRILL

The upright golf swing is an excellent drill for understanding and practicing the proper swing movements. This drill consists of the same moves that were discussed in chapter four. It simulates the

146

actual golf swing with an upright posture. The sequence of the drill is shown in Fig. 9-2. Here are the steps:

1. Stand with your arms extended to your front and the club parallel to the ground at your waist level.

2. Rotate your upper body clockwise. Start cocking your wrists and moving the club higher once the club passes your (original) right side.

3. Keep rotating the upper body until you reach a 90-degree shoulder turn. Now the club should have risen to your shoulder level.

4. Pause for an instant and then move your hips to the left while keeping the head in its present position. Also lower the right shoulder to drop the club to a lower plane.

5. Continue with the lower body rotation. Uncock the wrists and cross the arms to release the club once the hands pass the right foot.

6. Continue to rotate to the finish position with the club rising back to the shoulder level.

Fig. 9-2 The Upright Swing Drill

THE QUARTER-SWING DRILL

In a quarter-swing, the club can and should stay on one plane the entire time. The quarter-swing, therefore, is a perfect drill to improve a golfer's ability to swing the club on plane within the impact zone. It will also enhance his ability to sense the club position. In addition, it is a very important for your short game.

Keep the club on the NSP
all the time

Fig. 9-3 Quarter-swing Drill

The quarter-swing is also a good drill for maintaining the lag. For those who cast their clubs, the 90-degree angle between the left arm and the club is usually gone at the quarter-swing position. With the quarter-swing drill, the 90-degree angle is still in place at the start of the downswing. Since the golfer does not have enough time to lose the angle, his club will enter the striking slot with most of the lag. For this reason, the quarter-swing drill will help a golfer acquire the right feel within the impact zone.

A half-swing can also be used for similar training purposes. In this case, the club might come above the NSP slightly at the half-swing position but the range of plane deviation should be quite insignificant.

THE PUMP DRILL

The pump drill is a popular drill that many instructors have used for lag training. It is also a perfect drill to ingrain the key movements in the initial downswing: lowering the club to the striking plane. Here are the steps for pump drill:

Fig. 9-4 Pump Drill

1. From a golf setup position, set your wrists to so the club is parallel to both the ground and target line. Your hands can move to the right slightly.
2. Rotate your upper body clockwise to swing the club up to the three-quarter swing position.
3. Rotate your body counterclockwise to drop the club down to a lower plane and stop at the point where your hands are over the right thigh and the club is again parallel to both the ground and target line. In this process, *the lower body leads the movement and the hands and arms should stay relatively passive.*
4. Swing the club back to the top and repeat steps two and three twice. Then complete the whole swing in the third cycle.

The moves in a pump drill are also the initial downswing moves Ben Hogan described in *Five Lessons*: "The turning of the hips inaugurates the downswing. This movement of the hips automatically lowers the arms and hands to a position just above the hip level."

In the pump drill, it is helpful to pretend that you are trying to hit a wall on your left side with the butt of the club. You can also visualize the striking plane and focus on lowering the club onto it. With these swing thoughts, your shoulders and right arm will automatically get into the right positions. Your right elbow will automatically stick to your right side because it cannot go elsewhere. If you are a visual learner, there are plenty of pump drill videos you can watch on the internet.

FINAL NOTE

Golf is also a game of probability. Your potential score in a round reflects the probability of your misses: the higher the probability of bad shots, the higher your scores could be. To shoot low scores regularly, you have to lower the percentage of the bad shots through diligent practice.

If you can only hit a particular shot successfully 50% of the time during practice, the chance for you to execute that shot well under pressure can only be lower. To conclude this chapter, as well as this book, I would like to share a famous saying in sports:

> *"Don't practice until you get it right, practice until you can't get it wrong!"*

About the Authors

XICHAO MO

Xichao (pronounced as ['sēchaù]) graduated from Nankai University as a Master of Science in Electrical Engineering and is now an electrical design consultant, author, and entrepreneur. He had previously worked as a senior electrical engineer and the Director of Engineering at Hi-tech Electronic Displays, and later as a lead electrical engineer at GE Aviation. He started playing golf in 2008 and has passionately engaged in the research of golf swing plane and ball flight. He often uses Max, which stands for his initials M and X, as his nickname in golfing.

Email: maxgolf@outlook.com

DAN COURTNEY (coauthor)

Dan graduated from Golf Academy of America with honors and was a recipient of the President's Award. He is now the Head Teaching Professional of Don Law Golf Academy at Cypress Creek Country Club, Boynton Beach, Florida.

Made in the USA
Lexington, KY
12 September 2014